"In his concern to promote hea[...] Harvey ensures that we understand leadership pl[...], functioning team of elders in the local church. I'm not aware of another book that deals with this topic. *The Plurality Principle* is very practical and very helpful!"

Tim Challies, blogger, Challies.com

"Dave Harvey gives us another fantastic book. *The Plurality Principle* is enjoyable, biblical, and memorable. The fact that it is a quick read makes it all the more useful."

Matt Perman, author, *What's Best Next*

"God's design for the church has always been a plurality of elders—but that doesn't mean plurality is easy. Dave Harvey knows this, and he has provided this straightforward guide to help you cultivate effective plurality in leadership."

Timothy Paul Jones, author, *Family Ministry Field Guide*; C. Edwin Gheens Professor of Christian Family Ministry, The Southern Baptist Theological Seminary

"It is one thing to believe in the necessity of a plurality of elders but quite another to understand what that means! Dave Harvey does an excellent job of explaining it. He has put into words the reality I have wanted to share with fellow pastors as the dean of a church-based seminary—the type of fellowship that should exist within a team of elders. I thank God for this precious brother and the light he sheds on our path."

François Turcotte, President and Dean, The Evangelical Baptist Seminary of Quebec

"Every once in a while you encounter a book you wish you'd read years earlier. Having inherited elder teams in three different churches, I can testify that Dave Harvey's book would have been gold during those transitions. If you are a young pastor, save yourself the heartache of confusion and conflict. If you are a seasoned leader, it could be time for a biblical tune-up. The health of your church, your leaders, and your own soul might just depend on it."

Daniel Henderson, Founder and President, Strategic Renewal; Global Director, The 6:4 Fellowship; author, *Old Paths, New Power*

"Church leadership is the most perilous job out there, needing nothing short of the on-the-ground, forged-by-fire wisdom Harvey offers. From how elders can care for pastors to how elders and pastors can function together in practical, flock-sensitive, and Christ-honoring ways, this book guides elder teams through one of the most important needs they face: how church leadership teams can thrive in the complex challenges of real people, widely varying contexts, and treacherously subtle dangers."

J. Alasdair Groves, Executive Director, Christian Counseling & Educational Foundation; coauthor, *Untangling Emotions*

"Dave Harvey has done a great service for all who love the local church and have been called by God into leadership. He carefully explains why God calls local churches to be overseen by a plurality of leaders. And he steers us around the reefs and barriers that have left some church boards shipwrecked and their churches torn in pieces. By God's grace, healthy plurality in leadership not only is possible but can be glorious!"

Bob Lepine, Cohost, *FamilyLife Today*; Teaching Pastor, Redeemer Community Church, Little Rock, Arkansas

"*The Plurality Principle* will be of great help to any church eldership seeking to lead and care for the people entrusted to them. Dave Harvey has zeroed in on the key principles and has put very useful feet to them. This book will serve our eldering deliberations in the years ahead."

Mike Bullmore, Senior Pastor, CrossWay Community Church, Bristol, Wisconsin

"Being a pastor or elder is no small task. That's why I've found Dave Harvey's book so helpful. With a compelling vision and clear manner, Harvey makes the practice of developing a healthy plurality of elders both understandable and desirable. If you are planting or leading a local church and you want to see a healthy church last far beyond your leadership, pick up and implement this book. It may be the most humbling thing you will ever do, but also the strongest way you will ever lead."

Jeremy Writebol, Lead Campus Pastor, Woodside Bible Church, Plymouth, Michigan

The Plurality Principle

Other Gospel Coalition Books

Christ Has Set Us Free: Preaching and Teaching Galatians, edited by D. A. Carson and Jeff Robinson Sr.

Confronting Christianity: 12 Hard Questions for the World's Largest Religion, by Rebecca McLaughlin

Everyday Faithfulness: The Beauty of Ordinary Perseverance in a Demanding World, by Glenna Marshall

Faithful Endurance: The Joy of Shepherding People for a Lifetime, edited by Collin Hansen and Jeff Robinson Sr.

15 Things Seminary Couldn't Teach Me, edited by Collin Hansen and Jeff Robinson

Finding the Right Hills to Die On: The Case for Theological Triage, by Gavin Ortlund

Glory in the Ordinary: Why Your Work in the Home Matters to God, by Courtney Reissig

God's Design for the Church: A Guide for African Pastors and Ministry Leaders, by Conrad Mbewe

Gospel-Centered Youth Ministry: A Practical Guide, edited by Cameron Cole and Jon Nielson

Growing Together: Taking Mentoring beyond Small Talk and Prayer Requests, by Melissa B. Kruger

Here Is Our God: God's Revelation of Himself in Scripture, edited by Kathleen B. Nielson and D. A. Carson

His Mission: Jesus in the Gospel of Luke, edited by D. A. Carson and Kathleen B. Nielson

Joyfully Spreading the Word, edited by Kathleen Nielson and Gloria Furman

Missional Motherhood, by Gloria Furman

The New City Catechism: 52 Questions and Answers for Our Hearts and Minds

The New City Catechism Curriculum

The New City Catechism Devotional: God's Truth for Our Hearts and Minds

The New City Catechism for Kids

Praying Together: The Priority and Privilege of Prayer: In Our Homes, Communities, and Churches, by Megan Hill

Pursuing Health in an Anxious Age, by Bob Cutillo

Remember Death, by Matthew McCullough

Resurrection Life in a World of Suffering, edited by D. A. Carson and Kathleen Nielson

Seasons of Waiting: Walking by Faith When Dreams Are Delayed, by Betsy Childs Howard

Word-Filled Women's Ministry: Loving and Serving the Church, edited by Gloria Furman and Kathleen B. Nielson

The Plurality Principle

*How to Build and Maintain a Thriving
Church Leadership Team*

Dave Harvey

Foreword by Sam Storms

WHEATON, ILLINOIS

The Plurality Principle: How to Build and Maintain a Thriving Church Leadership Team
Copyright © 2021 by Dave Harvey
Published by Crossway
         1300 Crescent Street
         Wheaton, Illinois 60187

Cover design: Jeff Miller, Faceout Studio

First printing 2021

Printed in the United States of America

Unless otherwise indicated, Scripture quotations are from the ESV® Bible (The Holy Bible, English Standard Version®), copyright © 2001 by Crossway, a publishing ministry of Good News Publishers. Used by permission. All rights reserved.

Scripture quotations marked CSB have been taken from the Christian Standard Bible®, Copyright © 2017 by Holman Bible Publishers. Used by permission. Christian Standard Bible® and CSB® are federally registered trademarks of Holman Bible Publishers.

Scripture marked KJV is from the King James Version of the Bible. Public domain.

All emphases in Scripture quotations have been added by the author.

Trade paperback ISBN: 978-1-4335-7154-1
ePub ISBN: 978-1-4335-7157-2
PDF ISBN: 978-1-4335-7155-8
Mobipocket ISBN: 978-1-4335-7156-5

Library of Congress Cataloging-in-Publication Data

Names: Harvey, David T. (David Thomas), 1960– author.
Title: The plurality principle : how to build and maintain a thriving church leadership team / Dave Harvey ; foreword by Sam Storms.
Description: Wheaton, Illinois : Crossway, 2021. | Series: The gospel coalition | Includes bibliographical references and index.
Identifiers: LCCN 2020029741 (print) | LCCN 2020029742 (ebook) | ISBN 9781433571541 (trade paperback) | ISBN 9781433571558 (pdf) | ISBN 9781433571565 (mobipocket) | ISBN 9781433571572 (epub)
Subjects: LCSH: Christian leadership. | Elders (Church officers) | Group ministry.
Classification: LCC BV652.1 .H278 2021 (print) | LCC BV652.1 (ebook) | DDC 253—dc23
LC record available at https://lccn.loc.gov/2020029741
LC ebook record available at https://lccn.loc.gov/2020029742

To Wayne

Who needs superheroes,
with a big brother like you!

Contents

Foreword

REALLY? AN ENTIRE BOOK on why our local churches should
be led by a plurality of elders? Aren't there more pressing and urgent issues that call for our attention? After all, among the many
"-ologies," shouldn't we emphasize Christology (the study of Jesus
Christ) and soteriology (the study of salvation) and eschatology
(the study of the end times) and hamartiology (the study of sin)?
Is ecclesiology, the study of the church, terribly important? Does
it matter all that much?

My answer, and the answer that Dave Harvey provides in this
excellent book, is a resounding yes! I once heard J. I. Packer say
that "bad theology hurts people." So, too, does bad ecclesiology.
That statement may catch many of you by surprise. You struggle to
believe that the way a local church is organized, led, and governed
could possibly cause much damage. And yet, unbiblical leadership
structures in the local church can wreak havoc on the people of
God and bring reproach on the name of Jesus Christ. A failure
to honor the clear teaching of Scripture on how a church should
be governed is a recipe for disaster. Simply put, as Dave Harvey
repeatedly asserts, the quality of elder plurality determines the
spiritual health of a church.

One need only survey the landscape of recent train wrecks in several local churches to see how true this is. In virtually every instance where a gifted leader or pastor succumbed to temptation—be it sex, pride, isolation, bullying, or monetary misman-agement—the problem can be traced to a singular, authoritarian "pastor" who largely avoided meaningful accountability and built the ministry around his own giftedness and personality. I have in mind the sort of senior leader who never loses a vote; who regularly intimidates his staff, elder board, or deacon board; and who is rarely willing to admit that others might have greater insight and wisdom on a particular issue than he.

There are numerous reasons why I so highly recommend this book. Dave Harvey is himself a veteran of ecclesiological train wrecks. He has experienced firsthand what happens when churches fail to heed the clear teaching of Scripture. His wisdom and humility combine to chart for us a clear path forward as he deftly describes the countless reasons why plurality of male lead-ership in the local church is the most beneficial and spiritually healthy model to embrace.

This should not be taken as an indictment of every church where "the man of God" mentality or the so-called "Moses-model" of leadership is endorsed. Some of you reading this book likely attend a church where the senior pastor is the sole elder. I've known a handful of such men who functioned rea-sonably well in this capacity. In most instances, however, the deacons (or elders) exist only to rubber-stamp his decisions, and his unavoidably limited perspective is the only factor shaping the church's vision. Admittedly, there are always a handful of exceptions where, by God's mercy, an unbiblical model of local church life succeeds. But that is no justification for ignoring inspired Scripture.

One of the challenges in a plurality of leadership is the relationship between the lead or senior pastor and members of an elder board. Many envision the senior pastor as the "boss" of the board, while in other churches he is often "held hostage" and rarely permitted to provide the sort of leadership and influence essential to a healthy spiritual family. One of the many strengths of this book is that Harvey argues persuasively for a plurality of leadership while simultaneously making a convincing case for the principle of a "first among equals," a senior or lead pastor whose gifts, calling, education, and spiritual maturity qualify him to exercise a greater degree of influence and cast vision for the body as a whole.

Harvey's practical counsel on how a senior pastor works in tandem with a plurality of elders is nothing short of profound. Harvey does far more than simply defend the biblical reasons for plurality. He speaks directly and with great wisdom into the many concrete issues that arise on a daily basis in virtually every local church.

He rightly points out that the lead pastor does not possess unilateral veto power over the consensus of the other elders. He is alert to the dangers of a top-heavy, authoritarian, celebrity-pastor mentality. He is also wise in the way he warns against a failure to let leaders lead. He reminds us that a plurality is not an egalitarian enterprise that denies individual gifting, removes roles, or demands equality in function or outcomes. Even among equals, there must be leadership. And this calls for the all-too-rare combination of humility and courage.

Harvey addresses other critically important issues and questions with a balanced convergence of biblical instruction and common sense. He stresses the need for lay elders, provides practical insight on how much a pastor or elder should share with his wife, and speaks wisely on the sticky issue of how the lead pastor should negotiate his salary and benefits package. One trend spreading among numerous megachurches today is an external board of advisers that in many ways supplants the authority of the elders. Harvey's critique of this decidedly unbiblical model is alone worth the time spent reading this book.

I've been reading books on the structures and dynamics of local church leadership for many years. Honestly, when I was asked to write the foreword to this short treatment, I wondered if Dave Harvey would have anything to say that I hadn't heard countless times before. You may be asking the same question as you decide whether investing time into reading this volume will prove profitable. I assure you it will, far beyond what you can reasonably imagine.

As far as I'm concerned, this is the go-to book on the nature, role, and responsibility of local church elders that I will happily and energetically recommend to others in the days ahead.

Sam Storms
Lead Pastor for Vision and Preaching
Bridgeway Church
Oklahoma City, Oklahoma

Introduction

Why a Book on Plurality?

TWO DAYS AGO, the alternator on our car died. Back in the day (three days ago), I was blissfully ignorant of all-things-alternator. Now I know way more than I want to. For example, how much one costs. But I also learned that the alternator is part of the electrical system that powers the engine, charges the battery, sparks the ignition, heats the interior, and runs all the other electrical stuff in my vehicle. It's hardly visible and rarely comes up in discussion, but this unseen piece of machinery pretty much ensures that the whole car remains powered and moving forward.

A plurality of leadership—that is, a *team* of leaders—is like the alternator for the church. Most of the time, it's operating out of sight, and most people don't even know how it works. When it functions as designed, the church remains charged and moving forward. But where the functional plurality of a leadership team is absent, churches stall. Oh, and like alternators, pluralities can be very expensive when they fail. They require inspection and a dose of preventive maintenance. That's why my premise for this book is that *the quality of your elder plurality determines the health of your church.*

Looking in the Mirror

Shared leadership is about power, trust, accountability, and responsibility. As a result, it's relevant at every stage of ministry. But think about all the ways teamwork can break down. Maybe you are painfully familiar with one or more of these scenarios:

- *Plurality can be missing at the start.* Rico successfully started a church, but he lives confounded. "I've spent the last two years driving most of the ministry myself. How do I help our church become a place where the saints are equipped to do the work of the ministry? Where do I begin to transition this ministry from *me* to *us*?"

- *Plurality can be lost in transition.* Cameron was hired to be the primary teaching pastor at his church. The board of elders ran the hiring process, but now he feels like he's on the outside looking in. "I pressed the team on this issue, but they told me that they've been together for years. They just see me as the next hire; these men assume they'll be here long after I'm gone."

- *Plurality can be challenged in crisis.* After a leadership failure, Darnell inherited a large congregation, a functional facility, and a dysfunctional eldership. "As I've gotten to know these men, I've realized that half of them aren't qualified to be elders. Can we operate as a healthy team when half of the men shouldn't be a part of it?"

- *Plurality can be undervalued.* Reese is a gifted man, and no one is more aware of it than Reese. He can preach, understands organizational leadership, and seems to possess an innate instinct for identifying problems and proposing helpful solutions. The elders and other leaders around Reese feel pretty unnecessary.

Deep down in his heart, Reese pretty much agrees. When he was recently asked why he didn't delegate more responsibility, Reese observed, "God has blessed my ministry, and the church is best served when the plurality backs me up."

- *Finally, plurality can be ungrounded in reality.* Kyle woke to another day knowing the cloud of disapproval would shade his whole morning at the office. When he first accepted the role of lead pastor, the elders and staff were falling over each other in an effort to care for him. Now his flaws appeared in some form on almost every meeting agenda. Kyle was feeling crushed under the weight of expectations. What should a lead guy do when those around him confuse plurality with fixing all his weaknesses?

Every single church, no matter its governance, has to attend to the problem of plurality in leadership—to its presence or absence, to its beauties and absurdities. But we should see this as an opportunity. We all have plurality problems, but moving people toward a shared vision of doing ministry together is worth it.

Plotting Our Course

My first pastorate lasted twenty-seven years in the same church. For most of that time, I was the senior pastor, and we continually tuned and retuned our understanding of plurality until it served the church well. We made plenty of mistakes, and it was painstakingly hard work. It meant having men get to know me down to the level of my dreams, desires, giftings, and temptations. But I treasure those memories and the fruit that plurality bore in my life and in the life of our church.

Since then, I've served on various teams in different roles. Sometimes we've applied the principle of plurality well; sometimes we've made some big mistakes. But through it all I've only become more convinced of this key truth: *The quality of your elder plurality determines the health of your church.*

In this book I will share what I have learned about how to define, experience, and assess a healthy plurality of elders, and I hope it helps you. We'll look at what makes pluralities durable and what makes them so unpredictably delicate. We'll talk specifically about why and how a healthy plurality contributes to a healthy church, including

- how healthy pluralities keep the church moving forward,
- how healthy pluralities can be designed to work,
- how healthy pluralities create a context for elder care,
- how healthy pluralities offer authentic community that's characterized by vulnerability, honesty, and growth through self-disclosure, and
- how healthy pluralities, and the unity they enjoy, become a microcosm for the entire church.

Plurality matters. You see, the health and character of your team trumps the skill of the individual members. Ultimately, the health and character of your plurality will determine the health and vitality of the church. Together we will learn not to assume the health of our unity but to ask questions that will diagnose the strength and substance of our plurality. Together we will ask:

- Do we *agree* with each other?
- Do we *trust* one another?

- Do we *care* for each other?
- Do we *fit* together?

But it's about you too. A lot rides on your doing well in ministry. There aren't many vocations out there of which it is said: "Keep a close watch on yourself and on the teaching. Persist in this, for by so doing you will save both yourself and your hearers" (1 Tim. 4:16). Thriving in God's church amid the chaos of a fallen world is too difficult to be managed alone. For you to flourish, it takes a team.

My friends, we're not merely looking for a few laughs, a season of growth, some decent conferences, and a nice retirement package. We want pastors and churches that last. But to achieve that goal, we need strong pluralities. Denominations, networks, collectives, and local churches will be successful to the extent that they encourage, and help in building, strong teams. Why? *Because the quality of your plurality determines the health of your church.*

PART 1

────────

BUILDING A
PLURALITY

1

A Plurality Primer

IT HAPPENED AGAIN. Another phone call, another crisis, another pastor walking alone. My heart aches for this guy. Leadership has always been a lonely experience for him, dependent solely upon his highly polished gifts. I hope he sees the different path of leadership we discussed—a road less traveled but in keeping with God's design for flourishing churches.

Human beings are created for community (Rom. 12:4–5; Heb. 10:24–25). We're made in the image of God just as our God dwells in the delights of eternal community (Matt. 28:19; John 1:1–18). Yes, as God exists in community, we are made to exist in community. We are relational creatures who derive our existence, salvation, identity, and hope from a relational Creator (Gen. 1:26–27; 5:1–2; 9:6; James 3:9). This remarkable experience of community shapes what it means to be truly human. The theme of connectivity flows across Scripture and—to the particular point of this book—informs church leadership. Leaders are called to community, connection, and collaboration.

I would love to tell you that I came to these convictions by seminary study, by analyzing healthy church models, and through examining what's been most effective in the history of the church. Actually, my convictions began from a spiritual slap more than from anything that might earn me a pat on the back. This defining moment was a sort of holy headlock where the Spirit graciously grabbed me in my sin and pointed me in a different direction. Let me tell you about it.

Years ago, Kimm and I joined a church plant in the Philadelphia area. From the beginning, the church grew rapidly. Within eighteen months, I was invited onto the pastoral staff to help with evangelism, singles ministry, administration, and—well, you know—anything else that needed to be done. A few years later, some issues surfaced in the life of the lead pastor that raised some questions about whether or not that was a good role for him. Through a long and difficult process, it became clear that he wasn't the guy to lead the church.

Leaders are called to community, connection, and collaboration.

These events raised the obvious question "Who should be the church's next leader?"

At that time, there was another man on staff who had helped to start the church. He was a lovable, pastoral, fatherly guy who had been one of the church planters. Since day one of the church plant, his house became the center of care and community. This guy was a respected voice, and he possessed the love and trust of the people.

As I look back, it seems like a no-brainer that he should have been the guy to lead—at least until the church was stabilized enough to think more clearly about the future. After all, he was thirteen years older than me and far more experienced in ministry. Yet, instead of humbly advocating for him, I made too much of a certain weaknesses in him and resisted his appointment. Looking back, I had what the world might call remarkably high self-esteem. In Bible speak, that's a prideful and exaggerated self-assessment. I secretly believed that I was more suited for the role. In fact, I was stupefied that my qualifications weren't obvious to others! Pretty ugly, huh? It is to me. Even as I type these words more than three decades later, I'm still pierced by a stab of shame.

You see, the leadership vacancy gave opportunity for my jealousy and selfish ambition. The reality of my blindness was pretty serious, but my pride made me think my sight was sharper and more discerning than it was. As a result, I competed daily in the verbal trifecta of fools—speak often, listen little, never doubt. Maybe reading about me has you instantly nodding, because you have lived through a situation like this yourself. Perhaps you had a one-man show like Dave in your church. Or maybe *you* were Dave.

The good news is that God met me in a powerful way. But before I tell you about the experience, I want to tell you about how it drove me toward the Bible and the lesson it planted deep in my soul.

The Biblical Case for Elder Plurality

The Bible rarely talks about stand-alone leaders. Instead, it speaks of plurality. When I use the term *plurality*, I'm referencing the scriptural evidence that New Testament churches were led by more than one leader. They were, in fact, led by leadership teams. J. L. Reynolds describes it this way: "The apostolic churches seem, in general, to have had a plurality of elders as well as deacons."[1] Alexander Strauch agrees when he writes, "On the local church level, the New Testament plainly witnesses to a consistent pattern of shared pastoral leadership."[2]

In the New Testament, the term *elder* is used to designate an office to which a man is appointed—whether by the other elders or by the congregation—on the basis of particular gifts and character qualities he possesses (1 Tim. 3:1–7; Titus 1:5–9). Various terms are used to describe the role of pastor or elder in the Bible,[3] and

---

1 J. L. Reynolds, *Church Polity, or The Kingdom of Christ in Its Internal and External Development* (Richmond, VA: Harrold & Murray, 1849), chap. 9, cited in *Polity: Biblical Arguments on How to Conduct Church Life*, ed. Mark Dever (Washington, DC: Center for Church Reform, 2001), 349.

2 Alexander Strauch, *Biblical Eldership: An Urgent Call to Restore Biblical Church Leadership* (Littleton, CO: Lewis and Roth, 1995), 37.

3 The New Testament appears to use the words for "elder" (πρεσβύτερος/*presbyteros* and its variants), "overseer/bishop" (ἐπίσκοπος/*episkopos* and its variants), and "pastor" (ποιμήν/*poimēn*, literally "shepherd," and its variants) interchangeably. Three passages justify this assumption: (1) In Acts 20, Paul calls the elders (τοὺς πρεσβυτέρους / *tous presbyterous*) of Ephesus to himself (v. 17) and then, in v. 28, addresses them as overseers (ἐπισκοπούς/*episkopous*). In that same verse, he instructs them "to shepherd the church of God" (CSB), using the infinitive form of the verb ποιμαίνω/*poimainō*, which is a cognate of ποιμήν, our word for pastor. (2) In Titus 1, Paul appoints elders (πρεσβυτέρους) throughout Crete (v. 5) and goes on to describe the character and gifting of an elder (vv. 6–9). Midway through Paul's list of character qualifications, he switches to the noun for "overseer" (ἐπίσκοπος) proclaiming, "For an *overseer*, as God's steward, must be above reproach." Paul finishes the list in this verse but continues through v. 16 giving pastoral admonitions similar to those found in Acts 20:28–30, encouraging the elder, or overseer, to defend sound doctrine in the church as a means of protecting God's people. Clearly, that's what I call shepherding! (3) In 1 Pet. 5:1–2, the chief of the apostles exhorts his fellow elders (πρεσβυτέρους) "[to] shepherd [ποιμάνατε/*poimanate*] the flock of God that is among you, exercising oversight [ἐπισκοποῦντες/*episkopountes*]." This isn't an exhaustive list of the places where these terms are used together, but these three instances illustrate that when the New Testament authors write about an elder, an overseer, or a pastor, they appear

there are a variety of ways that pastoral teams organize in churches. But one key conviction grounds this book: *The New Testament terms for pastor, overseer, or elder are never used to talk about a single leader ruling or governing the church alone.* Instead, they are used to reference plural leadership. Here are some examples:[4]

- Elders (plural) are appointed to every church (Acts 14:23).
- The elders (plural) and apostles work together to resolve a major dispute (Acts 15:6).
- Overseers (plural) shepherd the flock in Ephesus (Acts 20:28).
- Paul writes to the overseers (plural) in Philippi (Phil. 1:1).
- A council of elders (plural) laid their hands upon Timothy (1 Tim. 4:14).
- Elders (plural) direct the affairs of the church (1 Tim. 5:17).
- Paul instructs Titus to appoint elders (plural, Titus 1:5).
- Peter instructs the elders (plural) as a fellow elder (1 Pet. 5:1–2).
- Peter tells younger men to submit to their elders (plural, 1 Pet. 5:5).

Passages like these bear strong testimony toward collaborative leadership within the New Testament church.[5]

---

to be writing about one interchangeable role. While this point does not forbid the separation of the role of pastor, a staff role, and an elder (a non-staff governance role, as practiced in certain traditions), it does suggest that New Testament churches kept these roles unified in one group.

4 Elder pluralities also are mentioned in passing in Acts 11:30; 15:2, 4, 22, 23; 16:4; 20:17; 21:18.

5 While I believe some elders should be compensated in their roles as pastors, I believe it's highly important that some are not. I'm also not overly concerned by churches that elect to use the title *pastor* for a paid ministry position and *elder* for nonvocational pastoral work. Others may choose to shed blood on this hill, but I will not. My years

We receive plurality as a gift—if we can only accept it.

Now, just to be clear: advocating the view that God assigns responsibility to a group of leaders is hardly a pioneering approach to church polity. Our Reformed forebears practiced this form of church government years ago.[6] Louis Berkhof suggested that it is precisely the practice of coequality among elders that distinguishes Reformed polity from that of other groups:

> Reformed churches differ, on the one hand, from all those churches in which the government is in the hands of a single prelate or presiding elder, and on the other hand, from those in which it rests with the people in general. They do not believe in any one-man rule, be he an elder, a pastor, or a bishop; neither do they believe in popular government. They choose ruling elders as their representatives, and these, together with the minister(s), form a council or consistory for the government of the local church.[7]

I believe Christ gave the church a plurality of leadership. We receive this plurality as a gift—if we can only accept it.

---

in ministry have convinced me its largely inconsequential, particularly when measured against the larger issue of whether they operate together in a plurality.

6 Samuel Miller wrote, "And as the whole spiritual government of each church is committed to its bench of elders, the session is competent to regulate every concern, and to correct everything which they consider amiss in the arrangements or affairs of the church which admits of correction." Miller, *An Essay on the Warrant, Nature, and Duties of the Office of the Ruling Elder* (Philadelphia: Presbyterian Board of Publishing, 1832), 201.

7 Louis Berkhof, *Summary of Christian Doctrine* (Grand Rapids, MI: Eerdmans, 1938), 589.

My Plurality Turning Point

When I felt called to ministry, I had no idea that being a pastor would become an essential means for exposing my sinful heart. Looking back on that early ministry experience that I described above, I can now see that I was undergoing a kind of open-heart surgery. I think what was happening in my heart is well described in James 3:16: "For where jealousy and selfish ambition exist, there will be disorder and every vile practice." Just think about it. I had an opportunity to partner with and serve alongside a guy more experienced than me—a guy who was trusted throughout the church and endowed with pastoral gifts. That was a slam dunk if there ever was one. But to my shame, I questioned his leadership and the wisdom of his appointment. My pride confused and corrupted me in an exceptional way. Anarchy reigned within me.

Little did I know these events were unfolding in a way that would profoundly shape my vision of ministry. My first experience of plurality—leading with another guy through a difficult situation—reached in and squeezed my disordered heart. Much to my dismay, what was inside my heart came spilling out. But that was the point. God had a plan.

If you're new to working with a team, you'll soon see how often plurality uncovers and forces you to deal with the heroic dreams and fleshly desires you have for ministry. When you think about it, this makes sense. To serve as part of a healthy elder plurality, a pastor must know his role, be willing to come under authority, learn humility, traffic in nuances that are neither black nor white, and be willing to think about his gifts and position through the lens of what serves the church rather than his personal agenda. Leading in community puts us under a holy spotlight. We have to learn to lead *under* some, *alongside* others, and *over* still others.

But it's all part of God's plan and protection. In fact, he will insist upon experiences of love or submission that will either break us free from our self-sufficiency or crush us beneath it. Plurality will expose our false identities, our preferences and prejudices, our high opinions of our own gifts, and our ungodly ambitions.

Had I known all of that back then, I'm fairly certain I would have chosen car sales.

But I didn't. Instead, God used that first ministry experience to expose my heart. It happened one day when I was sitting in the other leader's office. I was arguing with him—once again—over something irrelevant and unnecessary. At one point in our conversation, he stopped, became quiet and solemn, and gently asked: "Dave, isn't this just about your pride? Isn't this just about your unwillingness to serve and humble yourself before someone who may have more experience and be better suited for this role right now?" That's when it happened.

As I write these words, they may seem like the usual questions of a verbal sparring partner. But the words of this man's mouth had an arresting effect. God suddenly entered my personal space and authorized that twofold question as if it had been spoken directly by the Holy Spirit. It was one of those rare moments—and, quite honestly, I haven't had many— where the clarity of a simple question felt like the convicting voice of God's assessment. The man's words became a sledgehammer that broke open my soul. *This was about my pride, my self-glory!* A wave of conviction crested over me. I knew he was right.

Nathan stood before me saying, "Thou art the man" (2 Sam. 12:7 KJV).

A torrent of tears welled up within me. It was a beautiful moment, but I cried ugly—like a naked soul before a holy God. My greatest need in that moment was not to find the right role; my greatest need was repentance. I needed to humble myself.

My friend—I can truly call him that now—wondered whether this was some kind of breakdown. Should he call 911? Indeed, as I went back to Scripture, God was breaking down pride, selfish ambition, lofty opinions, and self-righteous assessment, both of me and of this other leader. My problem was not physical; it was spiritual. And when God flipped on the light, it illumined the road to repentance.

As an aside, I'm the kind of Christian who believes this sort of stuff still happens. In fact, I wish it happened more often for me, and I hope the same for you. But the most amazing thing about this experience was how God adjusted my perspective. God flipped my view so that I began to see things differently. In the days that followed, I immediately recognized that my friend was the right man to lead the church. And he did.

God's Purposes in Plurality

As we study the Scriptures, we see that a plural-leadership model is foundational for the local church. Plurality not only reflects the coequality, unity, and community expressed by the Trinity (2 Cor. 13:14; Eph. 4:4–6; 1 Pet. 1:2; Jude 20–21). It not only is, as we've explored above, the prominent and essential feature of New Testament church polity. But it also serves the church in at least six other ways:

1. Plurality embodies and expresses the New Testament principle of interdependence and the diversity of gifts among members of Christ's body (Rom. 12:4–6; 1 Cor. 12).[8]

2. Plurality acknowledges human limitations by recognizing that no one elder or bishop can possess the full complement of gifts God intends to use to bless and build the church (1 Cor. 12:21). This approach, in fact, discourages narcissistic personalities who look to exercise unique and exclusive authority or control within a team.

3. Plurality creates a leadership structure where men must model the unity to which God calls the whole church (John 17:23; Rom. 15:5; Eph. 4:3, 13; Col. 3:14). Plurality calls forward timid leaders to share the weight of governing responsibility.

4. Plurality creates a community of care, support, and accountability that guards the calling, life, and doctrine of the leaders (1 Tim. 4:14, 16; Titus 1:6–9; James 5:16). Where plurality truly exists, pastors and elders remain appropriately engaged, loved, guided, and harnessed together.

5. Plurality provides a mechanism to deal wisely and collaboratively with the institutional necessities of the local church.[9]

---

8 Bill Hull writes, "Regardless of what polity conclusions one draws, the leadership structure of the local church placed authority in the hands of a small group of men, not just one man." Hull, *The Disciple-Making Pastor* (Old Tappan, NJ: Revell, 1988), 78.

9 Gordon Smith, *Institutional Intelligence: How to Build Effective Organizations* (Downers Grove, IL: InterVarsity Press, 2017), 8, writes:

Pastors need to be encouraged to view the work of administration not as a necessary evil, a distraction, but as rather an integral part of what it means to provide congregational leadership. Indeed, if their vision for a vital commu-

6. Finally, plurality contradicts the idea of a singular genius and replaces it with what the Bible calls an "abundance of counselors" (Prov. 11:14; 24:6; see also 15:22) who collaborate, lead, and guide the church together. This isn't simply a clever constitutional maneuver. It's a recognition of the New Testament pattern. According to the biblical authors, the authority for the local church was given to the entire eldership, not just to one gifted leader. In other words, the responsibility inheres in the group, not the man.

The strength, unity, and integrity of this shared leadership model infuse the church with durability for its mission and care.

The strength, unity, and integrity of this shared leadership model infuse the church with durability for its mission and care. The church can't afford to sidestep this vital issue. Plurality is God's means of leading the church to fulfill its purpose, but it's also a means of growing its leaders.

The Rest of the Story

As time passed, my friend realized that he was not gifted to lead our elder team in a way that would ultimately be fruitful for the church. It was another mark of his consistent humility. So the

nity of faith is going to happen, they will need to attend to the institutional dynamics of church life—the administrative, financial, personnel issues of what it means to be the church. Their theological vision for what it means to be the church will be housed within particular practices, institutional practices that embody that vision.

senior leadership role fell to me, the last man standing. When I think back, the whole thing makes me smile. Some men are born leaders, others are appointed by vote, and still others have leadership thrust upon them. For me, I suppose I'm in the thrusted category—I was the only guy left. Appointment through the process of elimination! Suddenly several hundred people were waiting for twenty-nine-year-old Dave Harvey to get up and lead the next Sunday service.

But the story isn't over, because a few months later the original senior pastor returned to our staff. He took his place next to my friend, who had also been the senior pastor of our church. Somehow, in an inexplicable twist of providence, I inherited two older men, both of whom were ten years my senior and had already led our church. It seemed to me that this could easily become either a sitcom or a disaster flick—I just didn't know which. After all, these experienced guys were neither timid nor overly impressed with their new lead man. They certainly supported me, but they also had opinions, preferences, and clear ideas about how the church should be run. Somehow, we needed to find unity as a team; we needed to learn what it meant to collaborate.

For me, being the leader of this group meant thinking hard about God's point and purpose in plurality. I began asking questions like these:

- What does it mean to lead a church through a team?
- What does it mean to be a senior leader within a plurality of pastors/elders?
- How do you build a healthy plurality among a group of elders or leaders?

34

- How do you lead men who are older than you and have more ministry experience than you do?

Both of the other men were exceedingly patient with me, and their experience aided my training as their leader. Over time, I began to truly recognize a hidden truth about local church ministry. Sharing leadership with other men was going to achieve things I never expected. Our pursuit of plurality was neither an academic ideal nor a trendy leadership technique; nor was it merely a means for getting stuff done. Plurality was going to become an extraordinary means of grace for each of us—a grace that would deepen our experience of God, reveal our hearts in unique ways, bring clarity to our roles for service, ensure that each of us experienced genuine care, and make ministry a source of deeper delight.

My first experience of eldership plurality switched on the light bulb for me. That's when I learned that *the quality of the leadership plurality determines the health of the church*. I knew that failing to lead alongside these men would mean weaker souls and a weaker church. It would mean potentially forfeiting the mission. But succeeding with them would ensure a level of God-glorifying success in our spiritual lives that would spill over into the lives of the congregation.

And so our adventure began.

2

The Case for a
"First among Equals"

IN HER PRIZE-WINNING BOOK *Team of Rivals: The Political Genius of Abraham Lincoln*, Doris Kearns Goodwin tells about the exceptionally talented team that our sixteenth president assembled for one of the darkest moments in our nation's history. What I found most captivating when reading the book was the epilogue. There Goodwin chronicled the life of each team member after Lincoln's assassination.

William Seward, Lincoln's secretary of state, did well. Best known for his purchase of Alaska, he was a man of character who kept serving throughout the presidency of Andrew Johnson. Seward died peacefully in 1872 at the age of seventy-one, and his passing was grieved by friends.

Edwin Stanton, Lincoln's secretary of war, was different. Stanton's ambition made him acrimonious toward the next president, who eventually asked for his resignation. "Refusing to honor the president's request even after he was handed a removal order, Stanton 'barricaded himself' in his office for weeks, taking his meals in the department and sleeping on the couch."[1] Stanton finally relented and resigned from the cabinet. Years later, President Grant nominated the old lawyer to the Supreme Court. Stanton described that as the "only office" he'd ever desired to hold, but he didn't hold it for long.[2] Three days later, while his family gathered for the Christmas holidays, Stanton suffered a severe asthma attack, fell unconscious, and died at age fifty-five.

Salmon Chase, who led the Treasury department, saw Lincoln's death as a chance for new political life. At his first opportunity, Chase mounted a campaign for president, but in his first attempt he could not win his home state's primary. So Chase switched parties—on multiple occasions—to improve his odds. Though he later served as governor of Ohio and was even nominated as chief justice of the Supreme Court, he never stopped maneuvering for more executive power. He wanted the presidency. In fact, he ran for president twice while sitting on the Supreme Court bench! Chase ultimately failed at his highest aspiration, degenerated physically, and died in 1873. He was sixty-five.

Frank Blair's intemperate denunciations of his opponents undermined him in the public eye and cut short his political future. *(Those were the days!)* He was marginalized, and he died from a fall in his home in 1875 at age fifty-four.

Mary Todd Lincoln never recovered from her husband's death. She lived a miserable life marked by bouts of depression. She lost her youngest child to heart failure when he was eighteen. She

---

1   Doris Kearns Goodwin, *Team of Rivals: The Political Genius of Abraham Lincoln* (New York: Simon & Schuster, 2006), 751.

2   Goodwin, *Team of Rivals*, 752.

was estranged from another son when he dared to commit her to a state hospital after one particularly difficult season of erratic behavior. Mary died in 1882 at age sixty-three.

This group of individuals had something in common. They had a leader.

I could keep unpacking this list, but you should pick up Goodwin's book to do so yourself. Some of the people in Lincoln's circle lived peaceful and meaningful lives after their time serving the president. Others spiraled downward. But one truth stood out clearly to me as I read this epilogue. It became evident that the greatest achievements of the people surrounding Lincoln came not through their lives as separate individuals but through their united talent as a team. Individually, they were impressive. But together they accomplished far more than anyone dared to expect—winning the Civil War and ending slavery.

How did this remarkable "team of rivals" experience such unexpected unity and exceptional progress? It was because this group of individuals had something in common.

They had a leader.

First among Equals: The Unique Role of the Senior Leader

A cursory view of civilizations, both past and present, tells us that there's something universal about leadership. "But," you may say, "that is the world and things of this world. Life in the kingdom is decisively different!" I would reply that the world mirrors the kingdom when it appoints one to help the many. One could read Scripture as a legacy of God's activity in the world to bless and preserve his people, and he does this most often through the agency of human leadership. Throughout the Bible, when God chooses to execute his will upon the earth—when he forecasts the future, reveals his heart, frees his people, and preserves his purposes—he begins with a leader.

The Old Testament offers a gallery of names that remind us of God's regular pattern of using *one* to influence *many*—Noah, Abraham, Moses, David, Nehemiah, Jeremiah, just to name a few. In New Testament times, we're told, Christ chose the twelve (Luke 6:12–16), but he ordained Peter to fill a prominent role (Matt. 16:18). The Jewish synagogues were ruled by a council of elders, yet each council had a chairperson or "ruler of the synagogue" (Luke 8:41; Acts 18:8, 17). The early church enjoyed a similar plurality of leadership, yet it appears that James exerted a unique role and influence as the key leader of the Jerusalem congregation (Acts 15:13; 21:18; 1 Cor. 15:7; Gal. 1:19; 2:12).

The same is true in the church today. This is a book about plurality of leadership, but in order to make the case for the best model of plurality, I need to say that an eldership needs a leader. Now, I can almost hear you saying, "Come on, Dave, where is there any reference to a *lead* or *senior* pastor in the Bible?" You're right. There is no single, slam-dunk verse that decisively proves that pluralities should appoint a lead pastor. But there is a broad pattern of order—a beautiful tapestry of leadership—that appears from the opening pages of Scripture to the final words in Revelation. The necessity of a first among coequals in human economies is resonant in the way the Son submits to his Father in the incarnation (Phil. 2:5–11), as well as in the order God ordains in the home (Eph. 5:21–33).

Now, I want to be clear. A team leader—or, to use the common title, senior pastor—is not a call to headship over the team. Headship is confined in Scripture to covenant roles—within the economic Trinity, within the family, and in the church with respect to Christ's headship. But these examples—these patterns—still illustrate the notion that biblical leadership, though shared, is frequently organized around and facilitated by a central figure.[3]

Jesus was certainly an institutional revolutionary, but he did not renounce leadership. He just redefined it, placing dependency, service, and humility at its center (Matt. 20:25–28; Phil. 2:5–11). Though the authority for the church inheres in the entire eldership, a wise elder team will look for one among them with humble character, leadership gifts, and public ministry skills to fulfill the role of senior pastor. To this man they delegate the necessary authority to cultivate the unity and growth of the plurality, to lead the team into wise decision-making, and to help the elders

---

3   In the mid-nineteenth century, Reverend Eleazer Savage offered a Baptist perspective on this term:

> The want of united action among the different presbyters of the same church when they were all of equal authority, and the order of public deliberations requiring that there should be some one "invested at least with the authority of collecting the sentiments and executing the resolutions" of the church, led to the appointment of one of their number as permanent president or moderator. The title bishop, which was applied to all the elders, came after a while to be applied exclusively to the president—as Justin in the middle of the second century still calls him—merely to distinguish him from his equal co-elders. He was not superior to them, but only "first among equals."

Eleazer Savage, "Apostolical Church Polity (1874)," in *Polity: Biblical Arguments on How to Conduct Church Life*, ed. Mark Dever (Washington, DC: Center for Church Reform, 2001), 532.

assume proper responsibility and accountability for the varying ministries of the church. In present-day parlance, as I've said, this role is often called the *senior* or *lead pastor*. For the purposes of this chapter, I'll use those terms interchangeably.

Jesus was certainly an institutional revolutionary, but he did not renounce leadership. He just redefined it, placing dependency, service, and humility at its center.

Historically, the concept of a *leader leading leaders* has been captured by the Latin phrase *primus inter pares*, "first among equals."[4] This phrase reflects that pluralities are an assembly of coequal parties, yet each one decides to subordinate himself to a leader. Pluralities do this, as I've described above, because they believe the *equals* are most effective when they have a *first* to tend the team and move it forward. By submitting to another, the elders demonstrate self-emptying humility (Phil. 2:5–11).

Straddling First and Equals

This doesn't mean the senior leadership role always works out well. In fact, there are two equal but opposite errors that churches can fall into concerning this role.

4   James T. Bretzke, *Consecrated Phrases: A Latin Theological Dictionary; Latin Expressions Commonly Found in Theological Writings* (Collegeville: Liturgical, 1998), 96; Alexander Strauch says it this way: "Those among the elders who are particularly gifted leaders and/or teachers will naturally stand out among the other elders as leaders and teachers within the leadership body. This is what the Romans called *primus inter pares*, meaning 'first among equals.'" Strauch, *Biblical Eldership: An Urgent Call to Restore Biblical Church Leadership* (Littleton, CO: Lewis and Roth, 1995), 45.

Some churches err by throwing the accent on the first word of that phrase—the senior leader as "first" among equals. His place in line is *first*, his opinion *first*, his preferences *first*, his needs are *first*. These *primus*-driven churches can actually incubate celebrity pastors, or even entire leadership cultures, that are power-based and hardwired for command and control. For the plurality, the church staff, or the congregation, this can feel like heavy metal music at a funeral. Such an indelicate exercise of authority can relegate godly character and humble service to the margins, sentencing fellow team members to a fear-based and unsafe culture. The result may be a culture characterized by ministry silos, where each leader does his own thing rather than risking collaboration. At other times, staff turnover happens, as team members leave because the senior leadership is no longer tolerable. Or worse, no longer respected.

Other elderships err by throwing the accent on the second half of the phrase. An idealism of interdependence levels the leadership field so that team members begin to think that leadership and preaching are not a unique stewardship combination necessary for the team or church. In a world where authority is abused and increasingly disparaged, *pares*-driven models may grow more appealing. But, alas, they too fail the church.

I spent my early years in ministry in a network where the elderships were once unadorned with senior leaders. By all reports, it was an exhilarating season and, if anything, it nurtured a respect for the churches that endeavor to exalt Christ through a coequal eldership *sans* senior guy. Where you see this model working well, it's typically due to some remarkably humble elders. But in the polity postmortem for this style of ministry, the following observations were drawn.

First, a plurality without a senior pastor seemed to be structured better for protection than for expansion. In fact, this method of government is often most appealing to those seeking to guard themselves from the leadership mistakes of the past. This is no surprise; most polity is formed, at least in part, in reaction to past mistakes, experiences, and abuses. But this model definitely carried a trade-off—protection for productivity, preservation for progress. This means it works better at maintaining the past than for moving forward into the future.

Second, a plurality with no senior pastor often results in churches within a church. Pares-driven cultures miss a key lesson from history and humanity. People follow gifted leaders. An equality-driven culture may celebrate the purity of its interdependence of leaders, but in reality there is still someone behind the curtains pulling the levers. If there's not, *pares*-driven cultures will fade into ambiguity and paralyzed decision-making, or—worse— they'll spin out aimlessly, following the guy on the team whose opinion and personality is the loudest or strongest. Maybe you've seen him, the guy who is always entertaining but seldom wise. Or maybe he is wise but doesn't carry out the role of executing wisdom. My point is that since there is no one voice that unites and speaks on behalf of the eldership, congruent direction for the church is absent, and groups within such churches will often cultivate independent visions and identities. *Churches within the church!* Really, these are just cliques led by the respective leaders favored by various membership blocs. They just evidence that a church needs a lead shepherd to gather and move the sheep.

Third, a plurality with no senior pastor denies a legitimate avenue of service to elders with a distinct gift of leadership and a godly desire to bear this responsibility. Where power exists, it should be defined and identified for what it is. But these models often ignore the reality of power dynamics that push and pull the eldership. At least with a senior leader, power is more defined and transparent; it comes with the role. But a plurality with no senior pastor allows for unmapped and unaccountable influence where individuals cannot be held responsible. When power is exercised without roles, politics becomes a default mode for forward progress. As I've said, teams inevitably key off of the most vocal or most gifted elder. This man becomes a *de facto* senior pastor, but without the title, and this subtle slide toward the most gifted leader compromises the integrity of the coequal eldership, since his power is undefined and undeclared.[5] Those who work within this kind of parity framework struggle to act as one. Little teamwork takes place without a quarterback. Equality sounds great, but when roles are left undefined, it can be perfectly paralyzing!

Finally, a plurality with no senior pastor can create a vacuum of care for the elders. After all, it seems inconsistent, and perhaps a bit awkward, for any one elder to assume this responsibility. Yet care of the team, and of individuals on the team, is absolutely essential to the vitality and sustainability of the team. Senior pastors who ignore this are typically tutored on its importance through team

5   "Some churches claim to have a plurality of elders, with no single leader. But objective observation clearly demonstrates one person stands head and shoulders above the rest. While there may be accountability, debate, give and take on issues, the leader remains." Bill Hull, *The Disciple-Making Pastor* (Old Tappan, NJ: Revell, 1988), 79.

criticism, discontent, self-protection, or staff turnover. But care must be administered in such a way that it does not overshadow the mission of the church. Both the senior pastor and the team must remember that caregiving is often the default mode of pastors. But care can't displace the need for honest and courageous leadership, nor can it protect us from the risks necessary to see the gospel spread around the globe.

These are just a few of the obstacles experienced in *pares*-driven ministry. Admittedly, where the humility of an eldership is high, the difficulties of having no senior guy diminish, at least temporarily. But elders are shepherds who thrive on the active care and forward momentum of the flock. Restlessness, even exasperation, occurs when the pastoral burden is set within an inefficient or unproductive structure. After all, democracy protects far better than it propels.

The Beauty of *Among*

These two errors—the error of overbearing *primus*-driven ministry and the egalitarian error of *pares*-driven ministry—highlight the truth that to be healthy, the entire plurality + *primus inter pares* system must operate within a humility-protected tension. On the one side, the lead pastor must advocate for the opinions and involvement of the team as a whole, meaning that he must listen well as he obtains their counsel and understands their thinking. On the other side, the plurality of elders must create space for the lead pastor to actually use his gifts and lead. This means they grant appropriate autonomy (proportional to his humility and maturity), choose to be an adaptable and congenial group, and recognize the limits of each individual's giftings. The result is a beautiful blending of leadership and teamwork, where the elders remain jealous to protect the senior leader, and the lead pastor knows he needs the team.

Church leadership teams must understand that the wise senior leader, the "first *among* equals," inhabits the subtle space between *primus* and *pares*. He leads within the tension implied in "among." Straddling both first and equals requires both clarity and courage, elegance and diligence. Think art, not science. The wise senior leader is delicately dialing his leadership in the direction of *first*, then *equals*, then back again . . . without ever leaving the terrain of *among*.

You see, the lead pastor does not occupy his role because God sprinkled extra authority upon his life. In fact, he bears a greater burden. The senior leader becomes a steward of the group's authority *and* responsibility *and* accountability. At the same time, any temptation to believe his role is uniquely sacrificial compared with other elders' can be quickly disabused by simply filling the shoes of another team member. A father who makes assumptions about the so-called "burdens of dad" often has his assumptions capsized after swapping roles with his wife for a day. Effective senior pastors lead with awareness that it's often more difficult to submit than to lead. Winston Churchill's words should echo in the ears of every senior leader: "In any sphere of action there

> *Church leadership teams must understand that the wise senior leader inhabits the subtle space between* primus *and* pares. *He leads within the tension implied in "among."*

can be no comparison between the positions of number one and numbers two, three, or four. . . . The duties and problems of all persons other than number one are quite different and in many ways more difficult."[6]

So why a senior leader? Because elders work in the complicated world of people and decisions. In fact, elders will at times be divided in their opinions. For this reason, the lead pastor must be given enough freedom and trust to advocate a process and plan that stirs faith in the elders. By appointing him to the role of lead pastor, the plurality delegates to him an authority to serve the team when the team needs help in moving forward for the good of the church. But, again, *his warrant to lead comes from the plurality*.

Check out that sentence again. In fact, if you lead a large church, read it several times. I say this because there comes a time where the lead pastor may disagree with the elders' final decision but will nevertheless be duty bound to represent their position without hesitation.

It happened to John Piper.

When the leadership of Bethlehem Baptist Church arrived at their position on divorce and remarriage, John Piper disagreed with the elders about certain features of where they landed. You read that right. The doctrinal position adopted by Bethlehem Baptist Church was not the one advocated by John Piper—the modern-day prince of preachers—but the one affirmed by the *plurality*! Stop and think about that. Piper led his church through a process of affirming a position that he did not fully hold himself.

6 Winston Churchill, *The Second World War*, vol. 2, *Their Finest Hour* (Boston: Houghton Mifflin, 1949), 14.

But because the plurality of elders affirmed and adopted it, Piper was conscience-bound to execute the will of the elders (though he was wisely afforded the opportunity by the elders to explain where he dissented).

Here's the thing: John Piper didn't assume that his role as lead pastor gave him veto power over positions taken by the plurality. He didn't go to the final elders meeting on this matter saying, "Let's do it this way: Whoever around this table has sold the most books gets to make the final call!" While we are all more aware of the man with a respected name, a compelling intellect, incalculable book sales, and a global following, Piper knew that his role existed to represent the plurality, even when he disagreed.

The unique leadership role of the senior pastor requires developing relationships as much as, dare I say even more than, having gifts and skills. To become a joy-inspiring senior leader requires a blend of trust and humility. The lead pastor must have confidence that his team is willing to follow him as a strong-but-human leader, and the plurality must be confident that the senior leader is committed to serving with humility. Both must be confident that the other is willing to submit. And neither side must think it has cornered the market on clarity or truth. For a local church to flourish, it must see the beauty of submission and humility modeled between the plurality and the senior leader.

The unique leadership role of senior pastor requires developing relationships as much as, dare I say even more than, having gifts and skills.

There is little originality in this chapter; my advocacy for a lead pastor as "first among equals" is hardly groundbreaking. This chapter merely represents a humble attempt to recognize and apply the theme of leadership that flows throughout Scripture and history—from prophets and priests to presidents. I believe we need local churches that are distinguished by their order, innovation, and effectiveness, and I believe that local churches need leaders.

3

Dressing for Leadership Storms

Five Hats Senior Pastors Wear

MY JOURNEY IN MINISTRY and with leadership pluralities eventually led Kimm and me to Florida, a state where autumn is replaced by something called "hurricane season." Just think of summer, and then add torrential rain.

In this part of the country, good meteorologists are preferred over a good doctor any day of the week. Their currency is sky high and orders just beneath an honest mechanic. And autumn is their annual Super Bowl. Coconut trees will stoop to kiss the ground under the gusts of hurricane gales, but these intrepid souls will plant themselves in the middle of the mayhem, reporting what they see and forecasting what's coming our way. After all, the right call—a correct forecast—during hurricane season can put a meteorologist on the map. It's a *carpe diem* moment!

This chapter is a sort of meteorological message. It's my own emergency broadcast system for local church leaders. It's a report to help you prepare for the weather patterns making landfall on the shores of your church. These systems, swirling off the shores of Cape Leadership, portend rough weather for elder pluralities and, even more specifically, for the senior leadership role. As leaders today, we need to tune in and track just how bad this tempest is going to be.

Two Signs of Brewing Leadership Storms

Winds of Cynicism about Leadership and Authority

We live in an age of exaggerated autonomy and independence. People want to be independent from absolutes, and they're skeptical about anyone who inhabits a position of authority. Cynicism breeds suspicion toward all who bear the responsibility to lead. Accepting a call to ministry in this climate is dramatically different from when I started ministry thirty-five years ago. Back in the day, we might be offered discounts on food or services because we were clergy. It wasn't a courtesy we were entitled to, mind you, but it was sweet while it lasted. Nowadays, the weaknesses and sins of the church are so widely publicized that in many places the influence of pastors is only slightly above that of convicted felons. For this, we share the blame.

Cynicism is on the rise because the church keeps falling—and because media tends to magnify every failure.

But cynicism, be it mine, yours, or the sort that belongs to the latest cast of *Saturday Night Live*, springs from the fallen human heart. We can trace it all back to the garden. Lucifer was the first cynic recorded in history. "Did God *actually* say, 'You shall not eat of any tree in the garden?'" (Gen. 3:1). The cynic is always assuming moral superiority, always seeking to unmask dark motives in others. And, like the serpent in the garden, the cynic often attacks the way people experience and regard authority—whether that's the ultimate authority of God, the authority of his written word, or the derived authority of leaders, pastors, and preachers.

A culture of cynicism looks skeptically upon anyone who feels called to leadership. Rather than a form of service, leadership is increasingly seen as breaking trust with people, as compromising on democracy's code of equality.[1] For the cynic, noble advocacy for the equality of all people's value and dignity before God can morph and twist into the assumptions that everyone should also be equal in talent and position. The misguided idea is that everyone is equally gifted for every role, that everyone can *do* everything, that roles are interchangeable.

When a culture bends under this wind, a pastor's distinct call to exercise the gift of leadership (Rom. 12:8; Eph. 4:8–14) takes a beating. I've never heard it quite this bluntly, but the questions behind the cynical critique go something like this: Who would dare to believe they have a distinctive ability to lead others in loving Jesus? Who would dare to think they have the foresight to see the future more clearly and know what to do about it?

In this context, the appointment of elders evokes suspicion, and the very recognition of a senior leader lands like a conspiracy against the people. The hurricane of cynicism uproots discernment and development of the people. We lack the clarity, perhaps

---

1 "Democracy, with its alluring vision of equality, may encourage people to believe that every citizen is equally capable of governing and that no special skills are needed for this purpose." David T. Koyzis, "Does Tyranny Need a Twelve Step Program? Democracy and Tyranny Have a Codependent Relationship," *Comment*, July 13, 2017, https://www.cardus.ca/comment/article/does-tyranny-need-a-twelve-step-program/.

even the humility, to admit that others may have a greater body of experience. We lack the maturity to know that some have more knowledge or gifts that might better serve the church in moving forward. We lose the capacity to discern how to situate people in a way that helps them to be most fruitful.

Cynics often repeat the warning issued by Lord Acton to Bishop Creighton: "Power tends to corrupt, and absolute power corrupts absolutely." Lord Acton was absolutely correct about absolute power; it absolutely corrupts. But not all power is absolute. The cold winds of cynicism are brushing our cheeks when we turn these words against all forms of earthly authority and power.

The trouble with such cynical thinking is that authority is hardwired into the creation order. God made people to be kings and queens over creation. He mandated that they rule over his world (Gen. 1:28). Jesus is revealed to us in Scripture as the Son of God who empties himself of his preincarnate glory and prerogatives and submits to his Father (John 5:19; 6:38; 17:18, 22–26; 1 Cor. 11:3; Phil. 2:5–11), and we can assume that since we'll be gathering around God's throne in heaven, redeemed people will forever live within the borders of authority (Rev. 4).[2]

The implications are clear. Leadership is not a consequence of the fall but rather God's good design for human flourishing in a well-ordered world. It's necessary for humanity to be fruitful! To deny this truth is a clear sign of our cultural impoverishment. Wise leadership, whether by position or by influence and expertise, is essential for people to live as God intended.

2 I'm grateful for the way God has used the ministry of Andy Crouch, his books, and our personal conversations to shape my understanding of power.

Succumbing to Winds of Cynicism

Church leaders sometimes bend under the winds of cynicism; they begin to undervalue God's design for plurality in leadership. As I

Leadership is not a consequence of the fall but rather God's good design for human flourishing in a well-ordered world.

outlined in chapter 1, the decisive accent of the New Testament is on the plurality of elders, that is to say, upon the team and not merely the senior leader. Authority for the church inheres in many, not one. The church is led by a team and through a team. In fact, as we'll discover below, any authority the senior leader has derives from the group of elders he's called to lead.[3]

Admittedly, this results in some organizational and relational complexity. After all, if the biblical accent is on plurality, then it seems like leadership should be equally distributed. But that moves us back toward something like the equality-means-interchangeable-roles idea I've already discussed, and I still think that's wrong. A plurality is not an egalitarian enterprise that denies individual gifting, removes roles, or demands equality in function or outcomes. Even among equals, there must be leadership.

In fact, our diverse gifts suit us for unique roles. One member of the plurality may have a stronger mission impulse, pressing the team to consider the lost, both local and abroad. Another may have financial skills to advise the team on income projections,

3 Cf. Bill Hull, *The Disciple-Making Pastor* (Old Tappan, NJ: Revell, 1988), 84.

financial accountability, and how to budget wisely. Another may have the gifts to simplify the complexity of counseling. The beauty of plurality is that God assembles remarkably unique individuals to create a distinctive gospel culture. The absurdity of ministry is how often we miss that.

> *The beauty of plurality is that God assembles remarkably unique individuals to create a distinctive gospel culture.*

For our pluralities to be healthy, we need to recognize that while each man may approach reality differently, we together create a group personality. It's important that the team live out their diverse giftings harmoniously, with unity in Christ, and in keeping with a common confession. They can enjoy their diversity in perspective even as they strive by the Spirit for unity and maturity. And together they can help discern who is called and gifted to be positioned in the strategic role of "first among equals."

A Senior Pastor's Hats

Becoming an accidental senior pastor felt like being lifted up by a tornado and dropped into the middle of Oz. I wasn't in Kansas anymore. And as that realization dawned on me, I began to search around me for anything that resembled a yellow brick road. As a new senior leader, I had no idea what to do. The sheer height, depth, and expanse of my *ignorance* were breathtaking.

God had called me to this role. I believed that. Others even affirmed that I was the guy, but I didn't know what that meant. I didn't know what a senior leader was supposed to do. Our church had godly leaders who wanted direction, and they were willing to help. But I didn't own a compass. Or, for that matter, a map.

Have you ever left home and gone out into the weather unprepared? Or seen a TV weatherman do a location spot without first putting on his all-weather gear? Honoring the tension of being first among equals requires senior leaders to gear up as well. In particular, senior pastors must wear several hats. When each hat is attended, the plurality can function in health and strength. But when one is neglected, or several are, you may find yourself unprepared for a storm.

Honoring the tension of being first among equals requires senior leaders to gear up.

The idea of hats that I needed to wear is a simple metaphor for me, and it's handy, because I'm a simple guy. Maybe this metaphor will help you too. My goal here is not to list every responsibility that a senior leader could or should satisfy. Instead, I want to look at the things senior leaders can and must do to strengthen and empower the plurality they lead. If *the quality of our elder plurality determines the health of our church*, then we need to know which hats will best help us to cultivate solid teams. Here are five hats senior leaders should wear.

Hat 1: Custodian of the Plurality

The senior leader must consistently give himself to the health of the team. Each elder is charged to care for the others, but the senior leader has a unique call to care for the plurality as a whole. Lead guys, don't tap out. I know that some of you would rather be smothered in mayonnaise and tossed into a tiger pit than have a one-on-one counseling session with your associate pastor about his greatest fears. Note the word "custodian" above. The senior leader does not need to provide all the plurality needs himself. He is simply the one who is held accountable to see that the elder team is cared for. He's responsible, so he must work to create a culture of care, trust, affection, mutual submission, and genuine burden sharing.

I try to be sparing with sports metaphors, but this one was too good to pass up. Steve Kerr rode the bench a lot for the Chicago Bulls during the Michael Jordan era. That's no slam on Kerr; the Bulls were stacked with top-shelf talent. Nevertheless, Kerr said something about Bulls head coach Phil Jackson that should be said of every leader:

> What made Jackson special was that he cared about his twelfth guy as much as his best guy. He spent time with his players, bought them gifts, thought about what made them tick. . . . Jackson connected with them, sold them on the concept of a team, and stuck up for them when they needed him. His actual coaching—calling plays, working refs, figuring out lineups and everything else that *we* see—was a smaller piece of a much bigger picture. His players competed for him for many reasons, but mainly because they truly believed Jackson cared about them. Which he definitely did.[4]

Now, I understand that Phil Jackson is not a believer, and I'm sure there are colorful stories of his sinfulness. But common

---

4 Bill Simmons, "Appreciating the Zen Master in Full," ESPN (website), May 13, 2011, http://sports.espn.go.com/espn/page2/story?page=simmons/110513&sportCat=nba.

grace endowed him with some remarkable instincts. He cast a compelling vision of what it meant to be a *team*. From Michael Jordan down to the twelfth man, everyone was valued. Players played hard because Jackson cared about them—and, I suppose, because Jordan scared them to death! You see, the players weren't a means for Phil Jackson's personal agenda; no, he understood that a team is made up of particular people who must be loved, understood, and helped along to see beyond their personal game to the whole team. Jackson really cared.

Think about that, and then consider that coaching the Bulls to glory will only have earthly significance. The people to whom you are called—their conversion, transformation, and discipleship as part of Christ's church—live on for eternity.

Pluralities are kept not by grand gestures made once a quarter but through weekly examples of faith and faithfulness they see within the one appointed to lead them.

God has wired people in such a way that they pay attention to leaders. In fact, God has wired pluralities in a way that they do the same with the senior pastor. Does he encourage well? Can he see beyond himself to celebrate others? How does he respond when he feels like he has been sinned against? Where are his loyalties and liberties? Can he admit to being wrong? Pluralities are kept not by grand gestures made once a quarter but through weekly examples of faith and faithfulness they see within the one appointed to lead them.

Senior leaders are plurality custodians because, as the leaders go, so goes the church. This means that the work a senior pastor does in serving, loving, and shaping the elders often bears fruit within the church at large. The elder body often represents a microcosm of the church as a whole. Biblical imperatives that are not embodied and modeled by the elders will rarely be seen in the church at large. If there's not love, community, care, courage, or accountability among the leaders, for example, you'll have trouble finding such fruit among the members. Building a church requires building a team.

And building a team requires vigilance. When making a fire, you must remain attentive to the flames, lest they be snuffed out or, worse, burn out of control. Building an elder team is the same way. It's not enough to prepare and appoint elders. Once the team is in place, the senior leader must tend to the relationships in order to maintain a healthy culture.

Hat 2: Catalyst of Progress

Every elder works for two kinds of progress—personal and organizational. Each individual stands accountable before God to care for his own soul; a senior pastor must not lead in such a way that the other elders' accountability before God is obscured. He can, however, offer consistent encouragement and opportunities for growth. In this way, he facilitates the others' progress.

The senior pastor can do this in at least four ways.

First, the lead pastor sets the example, modeling how each elder should pursue personal growth. There is an active devotional life, an observance of Sabbath rest, a priority placed upon his marriage and family, and a humility when he is evaluated or admonished. I'm not saying that a senior leader should parade these pursuits.

Churches could probably use a little less of leaders talking about disciplines in ways that are subtly self-congratulating. I'm just saying that the lead guy should pursue these in private. The fruit will eventually speak for itself.

Second, the senior leader provides opportunities for the team to grow together. It's the wise senior pastor who arranges for his team to attend conferences together, study books together, work through controversial issues together, have meals together, hike together, enjoy parties together, and the list goes on. The senior leader must ensure that there are consistent structures and agendas for meetings, retreats, and training as well. If the lead pastor isn't organized enough to plan these things, he can delegate them to someone else, but he's still responsible. Intentionality is the key, since consistency in these things yields security in the team. Oh, and be sure to laugh together with your team. A lot. Do these things to ensure that you are united and progressing together as a team. After all, a culture of doctrinal growth and mutual support is not something many men inherit. It's something you must build into a team. Maybe the finishing touch on this point is to just say: Practice the golden rule. Lead your team the way you would want to be led.

> *A culture of doctrinal growth and mutual support is not something many men inherit. It's something you must build into a team.*

Third, growing together means evaluation. For the church to grow as an organized organism, opportunities for growth must also involve times of honest scrutiny. The senior pastor must avoid the temptation of thinking that analysis, feedback, or evaluation are personal criticisms. Even worse is believing that the willingness of men to honestly share them is an example of betrayal or disloyalty. A healthy plurality—and a healthy senior leader, for that matter—can debrief about meetings that went poorly, can evaluate preaching that needs improvement, and can measure mission effectiveness—all without getting defensive. That's how growth happens. And, once again, the senior pastor must lead the way. He must be willing to be an example in receiving critique himself and also fostering a culture where feedback is seen as a necessary step toward greater organizational maturity.

God gave us plurality because he's a big fan of humility. When a team is functioning well, we're able to own both our personal shortcomings and the shortcomings of the organization with honesty. Without it, teams and churches stagnate. They get stuck in the moment and are unable to break free to move into the future. At its worst, there is a culture of unspoken criticism where the elephant in the room remains invisible even while he stinks up the place. To identify the smell, we must be willing to humbly name the elephant.

To press the importance of this a bit further, think of humility like dribbling and passing in basketball. You can say that basketball is about scoring points, but you'll never score if you can't dribble and pass well enough to move the ball down the floor. A leadership team may have a shared theology and common goals, objectives, and action plans. But they won't move forward without humility. A humble self-awareness—individually and as an organization—

fuels and deepens our dependence upon one another, and it allows us to make progress with strength and confidence.

Finally, being a catalyst of progress means taking decisive action. Even healthy organizations will stall out sometimes—think of the unmet needs of widows in Acts 6. Even in the early church, people were neglected. The church needed the apostles to appoint new leaders so that the ministry could get moving again. Healthy leaders will listen, discern, and make courageous new decisions.

In all these ways, the wise senior pastor can be attentive to both his own personal growth and the growth of the organization. You can't trade one for the other. Focusing on personal progress at the expense of the growth of your team (or vice versa) will leave a team ill prepared when leadership squalls arise. But a healthy team, one where the lead pastor has ensured that the team is growing in humility, comradery, and strength, will stand ready when the hurricane hits. In the midst of the monsoon, that plurality will lean into one another. They'll find that the team's honesty and integrity can help the church weather any storm.

Hat 3: Curator of Culture

God embeds a distinct DNA in the cells of every church. Sometimes these genetic traits are obvious. At other times, not so much. Given his Spirit-distributed gifting and the particular responsibilities of his role, the senior leader is uniquely positioned to see the big picture of each ministry in a way the other elders may not. As a result, he's entrusted with a stewardship of this DNA across the church. Wise elders trust the senior leader to ensure that each part of the church reflects the whole. We cannot simply assume this happens just because each pastor attends the same meetings. Even if everyone is responsible theoretically, there must be someone who is responsible functionally. If you doubt this, send an email with a general request to ten people. Inevitably, all ten assume that someone else will respond. Where everyone is responsible, no one *feels* truly responsible.

On the other hand, leadership flourishes with particularity, that is, when responsibilities reside and inhere in specific individuals.

> *Leadership flourishes with particularity, that is, when responsibilities reside and inhere in specific individuals.*

Leadership confers "upon an individual the greatest challenge of all—acceptance of responsibility."[5] This means that each leadership task needs to be tagged to one person. No evasion, ignorance, or passing the blame can shift the burden to someone else. If you're going to lead a church, you *must* accept this obligation.

Yet the senior pastor must always remember that his ability to lead is based upon the willingness of the other elders to faithfully follow his direction. In response to Christ's humility, church elders are offered the opportunity to recognize the gifting and character of the senior man and defer to him. Stirred by their trust in God, their understanding of Scripture, and a desire to serve, elders set aside personal ambitions and self-serving agendas and subordinate themselves under the leadership of the senior

---

5 Francis Duncan, *Rickover and the Nuclear Navy: The Discipline of Technology* (Annapolis, MD: Naval Institute Press, 1990), 294.

pastor. In their doing so, the senior pastor becomes first among equals—not because he demanded, negotiated, or campaigned for it, but because his character and gifting commend him to the role and his co-responsible elders affirm this. The quality of his character inspires deference and submission.

Senior pastors do not exercise headship over an eldership, nor do they possess the right to elevate themselves. They should neither act independently nor create a subtle culture where hyper-deference to their wishes is the norm. The senior pastor is called to build a team, not a personal ministry. His effectiveness should be measured by the maturity of his plurality, not his social media following.

The responsibility of curating the church's DNA is fulfilled in two key ways. For one, it's accomplished by being a catalyst of progress with your team—by being *among* them and growing with them. In addition, a church's culture must also be cultivated by consistently communicating it. And that truth brings us to the fourth hat.

Hat 4: Captain of Communication

In terms of gifting and congregational expectation, the senior leader is often the one with the loudest voice. This is most evident with respect to the pulpit; the senior pastor is typically the most regular preacher. It must also be true outside of Sundays. The senior pastor must be the primary public voice of the eldership. That's not to say he is the *exclusive* public voice. A wise senior pastor will open up pulpit space to other strategic leaders, both from within the plurality and from outside the congregation; this not only allows the sheep to be fed from other shepherds but also grants the lead shepherd a break from his duties. But when it comes to voicing the culture—the vision, direction, and decisions from the leaders—the lead pastor must be the chief spokesman. He's the captain of communication.

That title carries within it a principle that makes this role, this hat, so significant. The principle is this: *He who occupies the pulpit steers the church.*

A while back, I accepted a call to a three-year role as the pastor of preaching at a church with another guy who had the title of lead pastor. The idea was that the lead pastor would lead, and I, the preaching pastor, would preach, and the church would think all was groovy. It was groovy, at least for the lead pastor and me. We enjoyed a great friendship, and we complemented each other's gifts in a beneficial way. But, for the church, this became confusing. They held an intuitive expectation that the vision and direction flowed through the preaching, and they were right. Fortunately, this church was also gracious enough to allow the plan to unfold. Over time, the lead pastor preached more, and I preached less. Eventually, the leadership voice was synced to the pulpit. Nevertheless, the lesson for me was clear: *In the eyes of the church, whoever preaches, leads.*

Hat 5: Liaison for Partnerships

In addition to these four hats, there's a final piece of senior pastor headgear that can help your church to weather leadership storms. The senior leader serves his local church by being a vital point of contact between the elder team and the church's primary outside partners.

The biblical call to interdependence is not satisfied merely by connecting saints to each other in the local church. Churches thrive by being vitally connected to other churches. Moreover, elder pluralities flourish as they recognize their need both for congregational perspective *and* partnership beyond the local church. Interdependence, both congregationally and through network or denominational affiliation, completes the circle of influence to maximize our strengths and bring aid to our weaknesses. Denominational or network partnerships serve and support the local church's mission to send missionaries, plant churches, educate future leaders, and advocate for Christian values and a Christian vision for social justice and religious liberty.

It would be naive and shortsighted to miss the fact that denominations and networks are made strong by supporting senior leaders, those who wear the hats described above. Since the senior pastor serves as the steward of the local church's DNA and as the chief spokesman for the plurality, the network or denomination's service to him—not to mention his support of other churches— is indispensable. A network, denomination, or collective has little influence within each local body without this robust collaboration. This does not mean he is the only contact or the only recipient of partnership benefits, but without his support and advocacy, these partnerships rarely maintain their place or importance.

In truth, extra-local partnerships exist because leadership storms have pounded pastoral teams and local churches since their beginning (Acts 15:1–35; 20:1–5). We've united because leadership in a fallen world is filled with complexity and opportunity. To supplement the limitations of our weakness and capitalize on the possibilities of our opportunities, churches lock arms together.

Our Rock in the Storm

But while I believe in such partnerships—they're the kind of ministry in which I've participated for three decades now—collectives, networks, and denominations are not enough to help you weather leadership storms. This fallen world doesn't merely need connectionalism. It needs a Savior.

Thankfully, the senior pastor is not the head of the church. Jesus is the church's bridegroom and head (Eph. 5:23; Col. 1:18). Ultimately, he's the senior pastor of the universal church. He's the chief shepherd (1 Pet. 5:4). He's the Father's chief communicator, the Word (John 1:1; Heb. 1:1–2). He's the catalyst of our growth; when we behold his glory, we become like him (2 Cor. 3:18). Ultimately, Christ must be our Rock in the storms of leadership.

> *Thankfully, the senior pastor is not the head of the church. Jesus is the church's bridegroom and head.*

When the tempests rise and the waves break over the rails of church leadership, we are not alone. We have help. For one thing, we have each other. And it's my prayer that each member of our pluralities will stand ready in the midst of the storm to help brothers and sisters turn their collective gaze toward the Rock. He's both our model for leadership and the Savior of our leadership. Relying upon him is the only way we'll weather the storms.

4

Counterfeit Pluralities

THE NAZIS' CODE NAME for the scam was Operation Bernhard. When conducted outside of warfare, the crime is called counterfeiting. During war, counterfeiting is just one of the tools of the spy craft and subterfuge trade. Nevertheless, the scope of this failed scheme was astounding.

The plan hatched in September 1939 when Nazi officials decided to forge English currency and then air-drop it over England. Their goal was to destabilize the British economy by flooding England's marketplace with counterfeit bills. The Germans hoped to weaken the British pound, drive up prices, and trigger inflation.

A Nazi officer named Bernhard Krueger was appointed to execute the ploy. Krueger, a former textile engineer, assembled a team of 142 experts—printers, ink specialists, financial experts, and plate manufacturers. This cast of characters all shared two chilling similarities. They were all Jewish. And they were all prisoners who were drafted from concentration camps.

By threatening these death camp detainees, the Nazis successfully forged 132 million British pounds, that is, nearly 9 million bank notes. Ironically, the money was never air-dropped into

England. The prisoners-turned-forgers slowed down their production time effectively enough that by the time they'd made the counterfeit money available, the Luftwaffe (the Nazi air force) no longer had enough air supremacy to make the drops and deliver the goods. Enough time had passed that Soviet forces now threatened Germany's borders. So, while some of the fake currency made it into circulation, it was not enough to do any real damage. For the English economy, the counterfeit catastrophe was averted.

No matter who you are, where you live, or what you lead, counterfeits always threaten you with catastrophe. Counterfeits ape what's authentic; counterfeiters present forgeries as if they are real. Counterfeits convince you that something of little worth has great value. Counterfeits defraud people and sometimes do so at a high cost.

We have some exciting terrain ahead. In the first several chapters, I covered what it means to build a healthy plurality, and we took a careful look at the senior pastor. In the coming chapters, I'll cover what is required to maintain a healthy plurality. But before we go there, we must address a hard reality. Teams can traffic in the vocabulary of plurality but not really understand the meaning of the word. Their lack of clarity can forge imitations—dangerous leadership cultures that praise the principle of plurality but misapply the practice. Out of such confusion can spring counterfeits, facsimiles that imitate the real thing. Here are a few of the common ones.

Counterfeit 1: The Expert-Dependent Plurality

I'm grateful to God for the array of specialized ministries that he has given the body of Christ. Every local church needs access to lawyers, counselors, consultants, seminary professors, and leadership or ministry coaches. These people, their ministries, and their spiritual gifts can sharpen pastoral leaders, supply essential perspectives, and help elder teams to wisely steward their responsibilities.

But these ministries exist to supplement, not replace, local elder teams. Parachurch ministries should also supplement, not replace, local elder care. Thankfully, most experts know they don't hold the same responsibility before God for the local church that local elders do. But it's not always clear that elders grasp this detail. Practically, this means that the advisors' expertise should never displace or expert out the wisdom, prayer, and deliberation of God's appointed shepherds. You see, "the Holy Spirit has made [them] overseers, to care for the church of God" (Acts 20:28).

But even when the experts understand that they are not primarily responsible for the local church, elder teams can cultivate the bad habit of making them the first phone call before looking to one another. This is not about involving wise counsel or even, when necessary, acting with urgency. This is about whether elders maintain the burden of responsibility for the church. Sure, I can think of pastoral situations where elders must act expediently in getting outside help, consulting a professional, or reporting a crime. The question is whether the elders then shift the burden of responsibility for the problem over to the outside expert.

> *Advisors' expertise should never displace or expert out the wisdom, prayer, and deliberation of God's appointed shepherds.*

Consider this scenario. Gospel Community Church (I just made up that name) needs help. The careful biblical exercise of church discipline has resulted in a lawsuit. Josh, their lead pastor, informs the elders that the decision on how to proceed will be left to their attorney. The problem is that the attorney will not give an account before God for the decision or the church. The elders will. Josh would be wise to involve the elders so that the decision is informed by both the lawyer and those answerable for the church.

Always remember that when it comes to leading a church, experienced professionals may be essential, but elders remain responsible.

The expert-grabbing tendency has become particularly acute with senior pastors. In fact, I believe this has been a significant issue with many of the celebrity pastor tumbles. Off the top of my head, I can list at least a half dozen high-profile pastors who, like the mythical Icarus, sailed straight toward the sun on the wings of their outside-the-church substitute for accountability. Some of these men certainly appeared accountable. But their self-appointed council of outside experts circumvented the hard-but-necessary work of letting the people who knew them best—those doing life with them—love and challenge them. Outsourcing personal care and leaving fellow pastors at arm's length undermines a critical purpose of the elder plurality: caring for one another. The greatest casualty of this expert-grabbing arrangement is authentic accountability. Advisors who look in from a distance can never replace the accountability of friends and co-laborers close at hand.

> Better is a neighbor who is near
>   than a brother who is far away. (Prov. 27:10)

Make no mistake: You can't preach about the importance of every-member ministry and congregational care while exempting yourself from it. In the defining moments of ministry, the elder plurality is essential.

One of the quickest ways for a lead pastor to undermine a healthy plurality is to communicate that the leaders around him, those appointed as part of his team, are not sufficient to care for his soul. It's nothing but rigging the accountability loop. You've seen it. The really gifted senior pastor convinces the other elders that the complexity of his needs as a lead pastor, or the unique pressures his family faces, or the quality of his gifting and intellect requires a higher caliber of counsel.

Advisors who look in from a distance can never replace the accountability of friends and co-laborers close at hand.

The jury is in on this practice. The verdict is "guilty of temporary insanity."

If Jesus was comfortable being called our brother, then no one is too great to avoid being a brother to someone else (Heb. 2:11). To use the words of 1 Peter 5:1, we must live as "fellow elder[s]." Again, I'm not trying to exclude outside help; I use it myself. But the gift of outside help is meant to be received in partnership with the local elder team. We must ensure that the men to whom we are accountable know how we're being advised by the experts. We want them to know what is being corrected, advised, and prescribed—even what is being seen and celebrated by outside eyes.

Counterfeit 2: Reluctant Pluralities

You know that you are part of a reluctant eldership when the members of that team don't understand their role or its signifi-cance. Each elder in a plurality possesses authority from God to serve as a shepherd, guide, and protector of the church. Each man is responsible to rightly apply the word of truth (2 Tim. 2:15; Titus 1:9–11). The plurality may delegate au-thority to lead pastors or directional/managing elders, and they may empower committees on occasion. But as a member of the plurality, each elder possesses an equal share of God-given authority for the church (Acts 20:28; 1 Thess. 5:12–13; 1 Tim. 3:5; Heb. 13:7).

Reluctant pluralities fail to act in keeping with the responsibil-ity they have been given. This means they are slow to evaluate ministries, meetings, or opportunities to work for the good of their members. Or, when they do, their words are so qualified or mitigated that constructive criticism often gets lost. This is not simply about the need for elders to speak more, though an elder who rarely speaks should perhaps reexamine either his courage or his call. But as with expert-dependent pluralities, reluctant pluralities rarely experience genuine fellowship or relationship with one another. As a result, they're often dominated by the strongest personality, and that is most likely the senior leader.

The wise senior pastor is one who recognizes that he needs the team to lead. For this reason, he works hard to level the playing field. Back in my lead pastor days, I remember being told once—okay, more than once—that I needed to be more approachable and receptive. Eventually I began to understand that my role made people more reluctant to be direct and honest. If I wanted the kind of help and perspective that I needed—the kind that would help me to protect my marriage, my family, the church, and my own call—then I would have to empower the men around me. I'm not sure that being easy to correct ever became a strength for me, but I think it was eliminated as an area of weakness. Senior pastors, if you're leading a reluctant eldership, it's time to accept your own responsibility to lead the change by freeing them to speak.

Reluctant elder teams may create the illusion of unity, but they can quickly devolve into an entourage of admirers so enamored with the lead man's instincts that they almost never dissent and certainly never question his perspective or behavior. Courageous men are willing to name nonsense when they first get a whiff. But an enamored entourage too easily becomes a group of enablers, a team whose mode of operation is simply to cut the leader some slack. It can devolve into pure pragmatics: "As long as the church is growing, keep your mouth shut!" Every leader must eventually realize that while overly accommodating team members may be great encouragers, they can't be counted upon to speak their minds. They may stroke your ego, but your back is exposed. When this dynamic is at work and unacknowledged, the plurality grows anemic, failing in health.

> *An enamored entourage too easily becomes a group of enablers, a team whose mode of operation is simply to cut the leader some slack.*

Counterfeit 3: Invisible Pluralities

Talented lead pastors risk making a particular assumption that can undermine the experience of genuine plurality. Here's the assumption: *the more gifted the leader, the less necessary the plurality.*

Let's not oversimplify this forgery or reflexively assume men with greater gifts are just more arrogant. It's more nuanced and diagnostically complex. Interdependence and collaboration emerge when a leader soberly realizes his limits and begins to sense that the wisdom and ideas necessary for guiding a church are beyond his capacity as an individual. In this case, sharing ministry with others becomes desirable, natural, necessary, fruitful, and even a relief. The conviction about the wisdom of many being greater than one man's genius seems instinctively correct.

Most of us dwell within a common and familiar range of talent. Sure, we're proud, but we also know we need help.

But the leader of many talents has walked a different road. Somewhere in his journey he's discovered that he grasps things more quickly than others do. He can diagnose problems more accurately, retain information more easily, express ideas more clearly, galvanize people more naturally, or win over a room with his charming candor. His experience has trained him to assume that, when given the space to lead and freedom to control, he can typically accomplish his goals. If you're a multiplication whiz, time spent waiting for others to arrive at the correct answer seems like downtime or even wasted time. You already have the answer.

> *The man who needs no one will soon be alone.*

A high-capacity leader may believe that he already has the best answers; the team is just an obstacle. Like the star running back who believes he can gain yards if he just has the ball, the leader forgets those blocking for him. Without the team, he wouldn't shine so brightly. Such delusions may last for a while, that is, until the star breaks down or the other teammates atrophy from lack of use or care. Here's the truth. The man who needs no one will soon be alone.

That sort of leader often emerges cultivating and then operating within a dangerous inconsistency. Plurality is certainly a good idea; it's just less necessary for him. Likewise, the plurality comes to believe they are less necessary. They slowly fade to invisible.

This is why gifted leaders can sometimes have difficulty keeping good people around them. Collaboration and connection seem inefficient; the other leaders seem less necessary, and their gifts less impressive. When a strong leader has a revolving door of guys under his leadership, it typically means he doesn't play well in the plurality sandbox. On the other hand, when a gifted senior leader can keep his team, it's typically because he comprehends his need for the other elders.

For a gifted man to have a strong plurality, he must be willing to walk a self-emptying path. This includes listening eagerly as differently gifted people provide perspective, analyze situations, express care, or even attempt to influence him. For people with unique talents and unusual qualities, collaboration may feel less like a gift for greater mission effectiveness and more like a restrictor plate on a NASCAR engine. In fact, it may well be *meant* to slow you down. *But your speed is less important to God than how you race* (1 Cor. 9:24).

A highly gifted leader who exercises wisdom will understand that he's called to more than faster and bigger. When leaders remain flexible and are eager to learn, they can adopt the wiser principle: *The more gifted the individual, the more essential the plurality.*

For a gifted man to have a strong plurality, he must be willing to walk a self-emptying path.

Gifted men can be more vulnerable to autonomy, lust for control, self-worship, and arrogance (Prov. 16:8; 27:2; 29:1; Luke 18:9–14; Rom. 12:3; Phil. 2:3; James 1:19; 4:6). But healthy collaborators hold up the mirror of godliness to one another and invite each other to peer intently at what they see. Instead of falling for self-deception, plurality helps us to see ourselves through the eyes of honest and godly men. An eldership becomes healthier when its members remind one another of their humanity, fragility, limitations, finitude, weaknesses, and ultimate need for God.

This brings us back to how God defines success. Success isn't rooted in our endowments; rather, it's revealed in how we humbly steward God's gifts among the community of his saints and before the watching world.

Beyond the Counterfeit

As a young guy, I once bought a late-model car at a cheap price. After driving it for a few weeks, I realized why it was so inexpensive. It was mobile rubbish, littering the highway each time I cranked the ignition. It was a costly lesson. If you want a quality product, don't buy substitutes. I speak from experience: counterfeits will only make you crazy.

A healthy plurality isn't easy and certainly doesn't happen overnight. It takes blood, sweat, tears, and humility—lots and lots of humility. But when you invest your life in helping to build one, you can stand on the deck of that painstaking work and discover that you inhabit a thing of beauty. More importantly, you discover that the eldership has become a powerful tool for gospel growth and church multiplication.

Leaders, authentic pluralities are worth the cost. Accept no substitutes.

PART 2

—————

THRIVING AS
A PLURALITY

5

Building a Culture of Care
and Accountability

REGARDLESS OF WHAT YOU THINK of the fortieth American president, Ronald Reagan was a witty guy—even under substantial duress. Some reading this may be too young to remember March 30, 1981, the day President Reagan was shot, but I remember it well. Semiconscious, he was placed on a gurney and wheeled into the emergency room. During that time, the resilient leader inspired the team around him by finding humor in his dire situation. As he came in and out of consciousness, he asked a nurse who had been holding his hand, "Does Nancy know about us?" When Mrs. Reagan arrived, he quipped, "Honey, I forgot to duck."

Finally, as he was wheeled into surgery, the president looked at head surgeon Dr. Joseph Giordano and his team and said, "Please tell me you're all Republicans." Dr. Giordano, a liberal Democrat with a brilliant intellect, asserted tenderly, "Today, Mr. President, we're all Republicans."[1]

1 David Emery, "Ronald Reagan: Grace and Humor under Scalpel," liveaboutdotcom (website), February 22, 2019, https://www.liveabout.com/ronald-reagan-grace-under

Leaders—even stubborn fighters like Reagan—need a team. In that moment, Reagan needed Giordano desperately, and the doctor did for the president what the best team members do. He engaged him amid an urgent moment, spoke the leader's language, communicated that he cared, and then he used his gifts—and his scalpel—to perform the operation that saved the president.

Four Essentials for a Healthy Team Culture

Leaders needs gifted people like that around them, a team that will demonstrate God's love through care, collaboration, and the scalpel of mutual accountability. In this chapter, my goal is to give you four essentials for maintaining that kind of healthy team culture.

Leaders needs gifted people around them, a team that will demonstrate God's love through care, collaboration, and the scalpel of mutual accountability.

Provide a Context for Care

A belief in caring for souls begins with the gospel-inspired presupposition that our ministry is only as healthy as our connection to Jesus Christ. Unlike other vocations, ministry flows from the inside out. You can be an accountant with a disordered soul. You can be a mechanic with an estranged marriage or with kids who think you are a hypocrite.

-the-scalpel-3299460; Peggy Noonan, "Ronald Reagan," in *Character above All: Ten Presidents from FDR to George Bush*, ed. Robert A. Wilson (New York: Simon and Schuster, 1996); excerpt accessed, https://www.pbs.org/newshour/spc/character/essays /reagan.html.

But, for pastors, the quality of our ministry is vitally connected to our spiritual health. Lasting in ministry means we must know our hearts and know how God's word speaks to what we see and what we can't see. To have a culture where active communion with Christ is cultivated corporately, we must both provide care for one another and also receive care from one another.

Note that word "provide" in that sentence. It's intentional. For many leaders, care is something they immediately expect from others. In my travels, I'm constantly running into leaders who are starving for care; they have planted a church or inherited a role and wonder why people just don't recognize their need and pour on the love. Personally, I love caring for them. In fact, one way I do so is reminding them that God has counterintuitive ways for creating a culture of care. Most often, it is built through the compassion, wisdom, and example of the lead guy caring for others on his team. The more he loves them, the easier it becomes for them to understand how to love one another—and him.

Remember, if you are tasked with building a plurality, care is not first a personal need to be met in you; it's a ministry that you supply to others. It's rarely a culture you inherit; it's one you must build. Teams are built, and a culture of care is conceived, when senior pastors follow this golden rule: "So whatever you wish that others would do to you, do also to them" (Matt. 7:12).

Here are two key principles we must keep in mind if we're building a culture of care:

First, the best care is local care. True care starts with those who know us best—those closest to us, those who know us well enough to track our joys and temptations. The guest preacher may look good in the pulpit, but his family and fellow elders back at home are in a better position to know the true measure of the man.

Recently I heard an interview with a fallen celebrity pastor who expressed regret over not having older leaders on his care team. As he described that ideal team, I also noticed he hoped to stack it with people entirely outside of his church. Here's a key take-away: advisors who look in from a distance can never replace the shepherding of friends and co-elders who are close at hand (Prov. 27:10). Outside help must not replace the plurality but must work in conjunction with local church care. I wrote about this in the previous chapter when I described the expert-dependent plurality (see p. 70). Outsourcing personal care and leaving fellow pastors at arm's length undermines personal care and accountability, two critical purposes of the elder team.

Second, local care is so important that the senior leader should own it. If this sounds familiar, it's because we touched on it in chapter 3. But it's so important, I want to expand on it here. If you want the local church to be a place of soul care, make sure the lead pastor is responsible for ensuring that the elders are receiving it. No one is better positioned to own this responsibility. The lead pastor can prioritize it from the pulpit, make sure care makes it onto meeting agendas, illustrate it from his sermons, and help build the church calendar with soul care in mind.

Let me say this more directly: Senior leaders, if your elders are not experiencing care, it's your failure. That's happening on your watch. But just to be clear, the senior pastor doesn't bear this responsibility alone. The opposite side of the same principle is this: Elders, if your lead pastor is not receiving care—or if he's constantly having to find it outside of the eldership without your knowing or inquiring about it, that's your failure. It's happening on your watch. And if he doesn't see the value in your care, then this should become a point of study and discussion. Do we, as elders, believe that for most of our life challenges, the word of God in the hands of believers (or leaders!) is sufficient for our correction and training in righteousness (2 Tim. 3:16)? Many leaders assume care should be outsourced simply because they have never truly experienced it within Christ's community.

Perhaps you're reading this as the lead pastor of a large church and now you're freaking out because it's physically impossible for you to assume care for fifteen to fifty elders. My point is not that you have to personally provide care for every one of your elders. My point is that you are responsible to ensure that it's being done. You must ensure that the systems and structures for elder care are created and that they are working fruitfully. You may even delegate the maintenance and evaluation of the structure to someone else. But you should always stand ultimately responsible for it being done.

You might be surprised over how many senior pastors—or, on the flip side, how many elderships—are all too happy to see this vital contributor to health delegated to professional counselors. They stand relieved that someone else is doing it. But they don't necessarily understand what they are giving away. Like a caboose on a train, care is coupled to accountability. Renouncing the responsibility for one has the unintended effect of losing both. Yes, doing care well and wisely takes hard work. Trust must be built; grace must be extended for clumsy mistakes; patience must be applied by all. But to enjoy true accountability and model the reality that pastors need to be pastored, we must place those to whom we are bound on the front lines of helping to interpret our hearts.

Remember, meaningful care doesn't just mysteriously appear. Leaders must take ownership and build it into regular leadership rhythms. Over time, as we invest in creating this culture of care rather than assuming it, a remarkable thing happens. When we intentionally reach out to other elders, open our homes, take an interest, and love those we lead, amazingly we also become the objects of their care. They care for us even as we've been caring for them.

Define Accountability

There's a common issue that can hijack a culture of care even before it gets started. That's the issue of undefined accountability. A team of men can provide a great service to one another when they take the time to clarify what it looks like to check up on one another.

> *Every pastor needs other men in his life who know him, encourage him, pray for him, and understand his patterns of temptation.*

If you're uncertain what it looks like to be accountable, let me suggest four values that we should seek to experience as part of elder accountability:

First, accountability requires being intentional. The best care is local care received from a community that knows you and tracks your joys and temptations. Let's face it. If a pastor's accountability isn't from men in his local church, it's probably not real accountability. It's an illusion of accountability where a pastor traffics in the language of accountability without getting entangled in its substance. Accountability requires having some defined and consistent context in which guys know you all the way down to the level of where your heart strays. Every pastor needs other men in his life who know him, encourage him, pray for him, and understand his patterns of temptation, where his desires are drawn toward soul-defiling pursuits.

Being intentional means saying, "I love my wife enough, my family enough, and the church enough, and I fear God enough that I'll be truly vulnerable with those appointed by God to hold me accountable. I'll confess specific temptations and sins to them. I won't share vague generalizations or use the sort of amoral language that excuses me from being responsible for my choices. No, I will ensure that these men know where I am most likely to drift. And I will receive their encouragement, questions, correction, and guidance as a means of grace to help me grow." Only when you make that kind of commitment can other men truly pray for you, encourage your godliness, and ask how you're doing. You allow them to press into the specific areas of your life that have the potential to detonate your family and ministry. And it's important to define exactly when and where these matters will be discussed. That's intentionality.

Second, accountability requires self-disclosure. While others are always welcome to inquire, it's not their job to investigate your temptations and sins. Rather, it's your job to disclose them to those who are keeping you accountable. It's their job to handle it gently, wisely, and with maturity (Gal. 6:1), not as fodder for recrimination. Fellow elders are not prosecuting attorneys cross-examining your life. The system isn't rigged so that the other men must always be on the hunt to uncover the effects of your fallenness. No, living an accountable life in plurality requires each elder to exercise humility—to open his own life to the others by sharing truthfully, freely, and happily with little or no provocation.

In Christ, we have God's self-disclosure (John 1:18). Jesus is God moving toward us and making himself known. When we're faithful to confess and disclose our own sins and failures, our own joys and struggles, we're embodying the posture of the incarnation in our own lives. We want to experience deep, accountable community and trust from others, but we recognize that the responsibility begins with us. So we move toward our brothers by making ourselves known first.

When we are principled about self-disclosure, the result is a more gracious approach to accountability—an approach that respects the other person's individual relationship with God. Behind the principle is confidence that God is at work in each person, propelling him toward a life of honesty before God and before one another. There's no need for us to be the Holy Spirit for our team. But there is a need for leaders to create the opportunity for accountability for their teams and for them to lead by practicing self-disclosure themselves. When the leader makes self-disclosure his responsibility first, it's easier for the others to ask him questions about his soul, his marriage, his parenting, and his ministry, and it's easier for them to share their hearts with him.

Third, accountability requires approachability. It's possible to be a gifted leader but for the other leaders around you to lose confidence that they can approach you safely with questions, personal problems, or criticism—no matter how graciously they offer it. It's your responsibility as an elder to make it easy for the team to ask you questions and share their observations. You should be generous and easy to talk to—even if the conversation is about something hard.

I love how Ken Sande describes approachability as giving those around you a relational passport (see chart 5.1). If you want people to let you into their world, you must first earn their trust with humility and openness. You know that you're approachable when others feel that they can trust you with their self-disclosure and with the care of their souls when they are struggling. Here's the truth: If you want to experience real accountability and helpful feedback from others, you will need to be known as one who is approachable and trustworthy. If you would like to know whether you are seen that way right now, just ask your elders. You might be surprised at what can happen when you truly humble yourself before the men around you. "God opposes the proud but gives grace to the humble" (James 4:6).

Chart 5.1. The relational passport

A passport is an authorization to go somewhere. There's no more difficult place to enter than the inner life and deep struggles of another person. If you want people to welcome you into their world—their real, messy world, not the smiling façade we all put up—you must earn a relational passport.

In order to gain a passport into the lives and struggles of other people, you must relate to them in such a way that they would answer "yes" to three key questions . . . :

- **Can I trust you?** Will you maintain confidentiality? Will you lose respect for me or judge me if I allow you to see how badly I've blown it? Will you be gentle and patient even when I'm exasperating? . . . Will you assume the best about me or will you jump to conclusions and blame me for all my problems? . . .

- **Do you really care about me?** Are you just politely tolerating me or fulfilling an obligation? Or do you really want to help me? . . . Will you take time to listen to me? Do you care enough to push past my outer defenses and take the time to help me sort out the tangled mess in my heart? Will you love me like Jesus does, even when I'm not very loveable?

- **Can you actually help me?** Are you competent to deal with my issues? . . . Do you have a track record of successfully solving these kinds of problems? What kind of training or experience do you have? If this problem is beyond the two of us, do you have the humility and wisdom to help me find another person who has the experience I need?*

* From Ken Sande, "Approachability: The Passport to Real Ministry and Leadership," *Relational Wisdom 360* (blog), July 21, 2014, https://rw360 .org/2014/07/21/approachability-passport-real-ministry-leadership/.

Finally, accountability requires a defined process of appeal. By appeal, I mean that the plurality agrees up front on the process for involving a third party if they enter into a conflict. An appeal recognizes that accountability is hard and sometimes needs help. Maybe the experience of fellowship breaks down due to a conflict that can't be resolved, or maybe one person in the group feels permanently tagged by something he's confessed. Maybe it's something more serious: you seem to be caught in sin and the group feels unable to help, or your wife feels trapped by some pattern of behavior you're exercising in the home and just doesn't know what to do. This is where there's value in including a defined appeal as part of the structure of your accountability even before you start.

To have a clear appeal, you must say, "We are agreeing that a plea for help may be necessary, and we are defining the person or group to whom we will appeal." Having an appeal says that seeking outside help is not betrayal or slander. No, it's sometimes necessary when sinners are trying to help each other.

Elders are human beings. Recognizing the need for outside help is just a way for an eldership to express their interdependence and open doors for discussion on their judgments. In a highly charged situation where the congregation or outside critics are vocal and polarizing, elders may feel political pressures to evaluate a struggling elder with less objectivity. If many elders feel the same pressure, the deck can be stacked against the accused elder.

Over the years, I've spoken with numerous pastors like Kyle— the lead pastor mentioned in the introduction, page 17, who lived under a cloud of disapproval—guys who felt like they were scapegoated through accountability processes. They felt their job was sacrificed to appease some interest group inside or outside the church. Maybe that's how things rolled; maybe they were not as innocent as they thought. But one thing is certain: where there's a defined appeal process, one group humbly allows its judgments to be weighed by another. Whether through mature leaders in the church, a respected network or denominational representative, or just a statured outside leader who knows the team, an appeal process defined in advance and a shared willingness to submit to it when the time comes to display humility, elevate trust, and help to suspend suspicion that the accountability process has a predetermined conclusion.

Having a defined way of appeal protects leaders and protects others from broken leaders. By agreeing to a process, the team members commit up front that they will not allow their lives, marriages, or homes to be closed systems—tightly controlled entities where they alone have access. No, even an elder's wife can appeal to others for help if she feels it's needed.

In Homer's *Odyssey*, Odysseus's journey home takes his ship past the island of the two Sirens. Knowing that the intoxicating draw of their call would be overwhelming, Odysseus instructs his sailors to stop their ears with wax and then has himself roped to the main mast. Bound in this way, Odysseus protects his men from any crazy or contradictory directive that might come once the Siren voices reach his ears. He determines before temptation how he should be handled in temptation. By deciding their actions before the Siren's enticements start, his men are able to sail past unharmed.

Supplying recourse for each other is a way to rope yourself to the mast. We know our hearts and we recognize that sometimes we will hear the wrong voices—Siren songs that may tempt us to contradict our convictions or change our course. We also recognize that in these moments of greatest darkness and temptation, we are far less likely to want or seek help. So we agree now (when we're sane) to protect ourselves (and those we love) from our own brokenness in the future. For the good of our families, our church, and the plurality, we bind ourselves to the masthead.

Meet Together Regularly

God loves us so much that he puts us into teams so we can experience care and hold one another accountable in ways that are fully loving and well-defined. But if we're going to practice care and accountability as God intends, it's essential that we meet together. It's this simple: for a plurality to lead the local church, there must be meetings.

That point typically elicits a collective groan. Many men I know dread meetings, feeling that they interrupt important work. But regularly scheduled, agenda-guided, time-respected, attendance-required meetings are part of what it takes to lead a cohesive and effective leadership team.

I've written in earlier chapters that shared authority does not mean each elder has equal responsibility over every area of the church. But this introduces an important implication for our elders' meetings: Each elder does not need to be equally involved in every decision. Elder teams can and should consider ways of organizing themselves so that gifts are deployed wisely, responsibilities are delegated, and meetings are attended only by the people who need to be there.

Moreover, the agendas for our meetings should reflect an understanding that elders are called to govern the church, not micromanage the details of church life. A wise plurality recognizes that its meetings will be most effective when the agenda is limited to critical matters, ones that clarify the doctrine and advance the mission of the church. Oh, and appoint someone who is not the senior pastor to chair the elder board. After all, being "first among equals" need not mean *obligated to lead every meeting*. Having other chairmen not only spreads out power but also helps avoid the appearance that the lead guy is really *the boss* of the elder team.

Having said this, I must also stress that when leaders gather, God is present, and he has his own agenda. We should launch into our scheduled agenda with faith and flexibility, recognizing that it's incumbent upon us to be responsive to God as he reveals his own agenda for the gathering.

> *When leaders gather, God is present, and he has his own agenda.*

Sometimes that different agenda is spoken through someone else's opinion. You see, when elders meet, their opinions are the tools of their trade. They are the instruments through which pluralities govern. This doesn't mean that every elder needs to express his opinion on every decision. As a leader grows more comfortable in the group and more confident in his role, he eventually finds wise ways of navigating the territory between saying too little and saying too much. But he must live aware of the temptation toward being a politician, that is, one who withholds his opinion to protect how he's perceived. Silence in the face of major decisions is typically counted as consent. If there's any doubt, the elder should be willing to speak.

In marriage counseling, we'll often say that conflict can be a sign of health; it means that both spouses are comfortable enough with one another to share their opinions. The same is true for healthy pluralities. Our discussions should be vigorous, and there should also be an awareness that resolutions and decisions don't always come right away. Elder teams should anticipate disagreements, even dissent. Dissent can certainly be a tool of the enemy to divide the church, but this shouldn't be our first instinct. Often, dissent reveals the strength and health of an elder team, not its weakness.

Though a clash of ideas can create a feeling of ambiguity, it sometimes pleases God for elder teams to pass through a crucible of complexity on their way to clarity and fruitfulness. In chapter 2, I wrote about how Bethlehem Baptist Church arrived at its position on divorce and remarriage. It's unlikely that the members of Bethlehem thought the eldership was undermined by Piper's dissent. On the contrary, seeing strong leaders who are willing to disagree while they humbly acknowledge that they may be wrong actually deepens the church's confidence in the eldership's integrity. This reveals to the congregation that the elders' public unity has been tested and informed. It's not predictable groupthink or merely a gesture or even an accommodation to the more vocal members of the team. Rather, it's the kind of unity that comes after vigorous discussion.

Can dissent be a sign of pride? You bet. It certainly was for me in those early years of ministry when I opposed the appointment of an older and more experienced man to be the lead pastor of our church. But the value of knowing where everyone stands is greater than the fear of falling into pride. Healthy elderships understand that dissent must be explored—even if it reveals the sinful heart of the dissenter, like it did with me.

Let's clarify one important point. Dissent is first an internal privilege exercised in the context of the plurality and its meetings. How it is expressed externally should be discussed and agreed upon by the elders. Sometimes a general mention of a dissenting opinion is appropriate; at other times, a written dissent may work best. But dissent should never become a piece of information that an elder privately relays to church members in order to gather supporters or to undermine the elder team. One of the realities of a plurality is that it sometimes makes unpopular decisions. In those moments, the elders must work hard to remain united. A plurality can't thrive if it operates like a bad marriage. When a big family decision goes poorly, one elder shouldn't point his finger at the others and say, "This was your idea." Few things can divide a church more quickly than elders who telegraph their disagreement with an unpopular decision of the other elders.

> *The value of knowing where everyone stands is greater than the fear of falling into pride.*

The elder team must agree that it serves God and the church first. Therefore, dissenters' names and opinions will most often stay among the elders. Unless the church would benefit from knowing the specifics of dissent on a decision, the elder team must speak with one voice.

Do Everything with Humility

Throughout this chapter, I've been writing about how meeting together, having a culture of care, and practicing accountability are necessary ingredients for maintaining a healthy plurality. In all this, there is one supreme principle we must never overlook. If you want to know the foundational secret that lies beneath great teams, meetings marked by unity, personal elder care, and lovingly accountable relationships, it's this: *humility.*

Humility is the oil that lubricates the engine of plurality.

I've said it before, and I'll say it again. *God gave us plurality because he's a big fan of humility.* As he says through the prophet Isaiah,

> This is the one to whom I will look:
>> he who is humble and contrite in spirit
>> and trembles at my word. (66:2)

When you consider all the ways God could have chosen to set up church governance, our loving Father must've had this in mind. Humility is all over the Bible (2 Chron. 34:27; Prov. 11:2; 22:4; 29:23; Mic. 6:8; Matt. 18:1–4; 23:10–12; Eph. 4:1–3; Phil. 2:3–4; James 4:6, 10; 1 Pet. 5:5–6). And plurality in leadership won't work without it. The only hope for a beautiful, dynamic eldership is found in making humility our aim.

God loves unity, so he calls us to a team—a place where we must humbly persevere with one another to function effectively. God loves making us holy, so he unites us to men who will make us grow. God loves patience, so he imposes a way of governing that requires humble listening and a trust that he is working in the lives of others. God loves humility, so he gave us plurality.

The only hope for a beautiful, dynamic eldership is found in making humility our aim.

With God, who always cares about our hearts, both ends and means are important. God has decided the church will be governed in ways that value humility both as the end and the means. That is, God values our decisions, but he also values the way we relate to one another throughout the decision-making process.

We're tempted to think that God's best for the church is what's most efficient, easy, and effective. But God's best is whatever is the most *beautiful*. And God himself, in the interplay of his own unity, diversity, and harmony, is our standard of beauty. God throws together diverse men with different gifts who have strong opinions and then insists upon their unity. As elders lead together, they're called to grow in their exercise of authority even as they remain mutually accountable to and responsible for one another. In fact, God is so committed to our growth that he appoints men in our lives who reveal where we need to grow.

Allow me to introduce you to Buster. Buster is a fictional character I use to illustrate all of the ironies of community. In this case, Buster is that guy on the elder team who is least like you. He always sees things differently than you do. More than that, Buster is the guy whose habits just bug you. He's the guy you have to work the hardest to love. And before you smile and chuckle out loud because you know who this person is in your life, keep in mind that someone else reading this may be thinking about you. For that person, you are Buster.

Now, here's my point: God put Buster on your team to help you grow. He's part of God's project for your life. Do you know how you love to be respected? Well, Buster is going to disrespect you. In fact, he'll often speak with a complete lack of awareness about how things land for you. Do you know how you want to feel needed? Well, you're never going to hear it from Buster, because he doesn't need you. And, when you do hear from him, it'll probably be something critical—or at least feel critical. But you know what? Buster is God's gift to you. Do you know why? Because unlike those who praise you constantly, Buster reveals how much you need the praise of people, or how hard it is for you to show grace to people who don't defer to you. In other words, Buster shows you what you really love.

Always remember: the plurality is not about your comfort; it's about your growth in godliness to better love and lead God's people. Sure, the guys on your elder team with whom you love to chill will make you grateful. But Buster will make you godly. In fact, Buster will teach you the gospel. Because with him, you have to work harder to apply it; you must work harder to love him. And that makes you more like Jesus.

Looking beyond Plurality

There comes a day when, like Ronald Reagan, every leader moves to the center of the crosshairs—not literally, by the way, but certainly spiritually and emotionally. How will you survive when the bullets are fired? One of God's gifts when it seems like we're going down is a healthy team—one that is able to identify with us, communicate that they care, and then use their gifts, like scalpels, to perform the necessary operation. This doesn't always look or feel loving in the moment, but God makes all things beautiful in his time (Eccles. 3:11). God wants to use difficult meetings as well as painfully clear accountability to show you his enduring love and astonishing care. And when you humbly submit to it, he'll use those seasons to do a miraculous operation—one that prepares you for the next season of leadership and, ultimately, to dwell happily in your heavenly home.

6

Acknowledging and
Sharing Power

BACK IN THE GLORY DAYS, I fancied myself a decent racquetball player. I played in a league or two, and I did fairly well. Unfortunately, this early success resulted in an exaggerated perception of my abilities, a chronic problem for me as, well, a guy. I was dwelling comfortably in the bliss of my ignorance until a friend in our church invited me to join him for a game. I sized this guy up, and I figured that I could teach him a thing or two. On the appointed day, we played.

The first time I saw this guy hit the ball, my world changed. Never in my life had I seen someone hit a racquetball so hard that it cried. After our first volley, my self-assessment shifted gears violently with no clutch. My game strategy spontaneously changed—from competing to surviving. I was tempted to curl up in a fetal position just to stay out the path of his shots. After my friend effortlessly won every game, he began telling me that he regularly played people who destroyed him on the court. I remember thinking, *Okay, there's a whole world of racquetball of which I know not—an entire universe of court play the likes of which I'd never even conceived.* To me, it was unfathomable. And, to be honest, humbling.

It's a good thing for a man to discover what league he plays in.

The apostle Paul played in a league of his own. When you've seen the risen Christ, penned Scripture, and ascended to the third heaven, then, well, let's just say you're in a unique class. There's only one Saul of Tarsus in redemptive history. If you think you play in his league, read the book of Acts again. Slowly, this time.

But here's something that fascinates me. Once we recognize Paul's unique place in the Bible and his distinct apostolic authority, it's astonishing to observe the way he gave away power. Rather than always centralizing his authority or sharing it only with those who immediately benefitted from his ministry, Paul spread power around. Or perhaps it's better to say that he pushed it down. He started new churches, raised up leaders, and empowered elders. Paul trained young men and then gave away his ministry to them. He sent friends like Onesimus away even when it appeared that keeping them around would have served his best interests (Philem. 10–13). Instead of claiming his right to Timothy's and Epaphroditus's help, Paul sent them back to the Philippians (Phil. 2:19–30). Instead of growing a financial base for his ministry, Paul worked as a tentmaker. Instead of expecting to be served—the typical prerogative of power—he served.

When it comes to building leaders and pluralities, I think Paul understood something we often miss about power.

What Is Power?

Let's fess up about something. We don't like to think of the power church leaders have. It doesn't seem spiritual. It seems carnal, earthly, and worldly. When we talk about power, we feel like we're wandering into secular fields where the world plays. But there's so much more to power than its corruption—more than dictators, dirty politics, and domineering bosses. And when we avoid talking about power dynamics in the church—when we over-spiritualize the fallen realities of leadership—we're being clumsy or neglectful, or worse.

In his book *Playing God: Redeeming the Gift of Power*, Andy Crouch tells the story of a journalist who interviewed the pastor of a multi-thousand-member megachurch. The journalist asked, "How do you handle the power that comes with the role you have as senior pastor?" The pastor immediately responded: "Oh, power is not a problem at our church. We are all servant leaders here."[1]

Now, from one perspective, we can appreciate this response. There's a humble cultural instinct to pivot from the topic of power to Christ's call for all leaders to serve. But, frankly, when we consider the pastoral authority attached to ministry, the influence that accompanies preaching, the impact of book sales for those who write, and the number of jobs that depend upon the leadership of the average megachurch pastor, this man's lack of awareness that power could be a problem was a little shocking. Andy goes on to describe how this pastor was drenched in gravitas: "I have been in rooms when he walked in and have felt the palpable change in atmosphere, as if someone had abruptly turned down the thermostat and shut off the background music."[2]

---

1   Andy Crouch, *Playing God: Redeeming the Gift of Power* (Downers Grove, IL: Inter-Varsity Press, 2013), 10.
2   Crouch, *Playing God*, 10.

God had entrusted this leader with enormous power. The only question was whether he'd deny it or see it as a gift to be used for God's glory.

Frankly, when it comes to power dynamics, "the sons of this world are more shrewd in dealing with their own generation than the sons of light" (Luke 16:8). Some businesses and nonprofits readily comprehend what the church often misses: the most durable organizations are the ones that see not single pieces but the big picture of power. Writing about how churches should respond to allegations of abuse, Pastor Chris Mole says:

> Several years ago while teaching at a conference in Indiana I saw something I had never seen before. It was an entire train . . . in motion. Now I know that doesn't sound all that significant but where I'm from (West Virginia) you never see the entire train. We have far too many obstructions like mountains, rivers, and winding terrain. I bring that up because cases of abuse are similar in that you rarely see the entire train; that is, we only catch glimpses of the abuse. We rarely hear of every incident, and will never really comprehend the total impact of abuse. That is one of the reasons many definitions of abuse highlight the existence of a pattern of abusive behavior.
>
> When I've seen cases mismanaged in either the church or the culture, one of the most common elements is a focus on a single incident or an event. This event-oriented approach can limit our vision and enable the abuser by narrowing his responsibility to confessing and repenting of one act, or one specific tactic, leaving the rest of the abuse train, as it were, continuing down the track. I often say that if we only address the event,

incident, or presenting problem, we risk empowering "polite" abusers who commit more covert, or even respectable sins.[3]

The sad truth is that churches have a history of granting free passes to powerful people—whether a battering spouse in a marriage or a leader who abuses his position of authority. When we see the person's momentary humility and come under the sway of his, "Aw, shucks" confession, it's easy to make forgiveness mean things that God never intended. After all, when power isn't talked about in the church, how can it be mapped? If power isn't identified by intentional and discernable accountability structures, how can we know when it's abused?

Crouch defines power as "our ability to make something of the world."[4] He argues that the living God opens history with acts of power: *Let there be light. Let there be water. Let there be land. Let there be plants* (Gen. 1:3–11). But then we see something unexpected. There is a delegation of power and authority away from God to his image bearers, male and female together, as they are commanded to be fruitful, multiply, subdue, and have dominion over the earth (Gen. 1:22–28). God now expects all human persons to exercise their power, that is, to use their gifts, abilities, leadership, innovation, and influence in order to promote the flourishing of his world. Having power involves having the capacity to create and the impulse to share and reproduce. As people faithfully apply themselves to God's creation mandate, their power grows.

3 Chris Moles, "Key Responses to Physical Abuse," in *Becoming a Church That Cares Well for the Abused Handbook*, ed. Brad Hambrick (Nashville: B&H, 2019), 79.
4 Crouch, *Playing God*, 17

THRIVING AS A PLURALITY

The wise leader acknowledges his power, knowing that power can corrupt with lightning speed when we're willfully blind to its presence.

Think about it. Whether you are Steve Jobs, Martha Stewart, Kendrick Lamar, Tom Brady, or Tim Keller, the more effective you are at "making something of the world," the more influence and power you gather. Even if a leader denies it, this doesn't diminish its reality. And while most leaders don't have the influence of a megachurch pastor, if you open your Bible to preach Sunday after Sunday, to counsel congregants, or to lead a church ministry, you have power and authority in the eyes of those you lead. As leaders seeking to build healthy churches, we can't act as if it isn't present. Denying our power only makes us more prone to misusing it. We must stop wrapping ourselves in the naivete that assumes a vocabulary of humble spirituality is the same as divesting our power. The wise leader acknowledges his power and leverages it wisely, knowing that power can corrupt with lightning speed when we're willfully blind to its presence (see chart 6.1).

Chart 6.1. Sources of power

Peter Scazzero writes, "A critical need for every leader is to become aware of their power, i.e. their capacity to influence, and stewarding that power well so they are a gift to those they serve, enabling them to come more fully alive and flourish."* But few leaders are aware of, let alone reflect upon, the nature of their God-given power.

This is essential for pluralities, because we all have power. Spend a few moments reflecting upon the following sources of power.†

- *Positional power* comes with a position or title. A specific role such as pastor, director, board member, small group leader, chief financial officer, or worship pastor provides a platform for influencing others.

- *Personal power* is related to the unique gifts, capacities, personalities, and competencies that God has given us. It comes from what we do with what God has created us to be.

- *"God factor" power* is related to the sacred weight we carry when we're formally placed in positions to represent God. Every pastor or elder carries this power, because we serve people in Jesus's name.

- *Projected power* is the power other people unconsciously impute to us. When others project onto us their unmet needs or unresolved issues in hopes we will meet or resolve them, this gives us power. Being aware of this power guards us against taking advantage of others who are needy and vulnerable.

- *Relational power* is power that grows over time in ministry as people entrust to us their fears and secrets. When we counsel others and listen to their secrets or painful experiences, they are trusting us. This adds to our power as we stand with people in their most vulnerable moments.

- *Cultural Power* stems from our age, race, gender, and ethnicity. Some cultures grant more power to those of advanced age. Sadly, the color of one's skin and/or ethnicity conveys a greater or lesser amount of power, depending on the geographic or social context within which you are ministering.

Take a moment to do an inventory of your power. Reflect upon each of the sources of power and the level of influence that each gives you.

* Peter Scazzero, *Emotionally Healthy Leader: How Transforming Your Inner Life Will Deeply Transform Your Church, Team, and the World* (Grand Rapids, MI: Zondervan, 2015), 250.

† I am summarizing Scazzero, *Emotionally Healthy Leader*, 245–47.

Here's the point. Wise pluralities have *power dynamics* as a functional category for how their leadership affects the church. They are deliberate and transparent on how power is exercised within their governance. An awareness of power differentials should influence our policies and procedures, how we relate to the opposite sex, how we set salaries, and—perhaps most important—how we set up accountability structures. In the previous chapter, I described an interview that I recently heard with a fallen celebrity pastor whose accountability dream team was stacked with people exclusively outside his local church. As I listened to that interview, my heart went out to this guy. I've served in places where authority and accountability structures were unclear and undefined. I remember the confusion and mess this created.

Pushing Out Power: Lay Elders Are Not the JV Team

My leadership teeth were cut in a denomination where lay elders didn't exist.[5] It wasn't simply that our tithing base provided the luxury of full-time pastor-shepherds. Rather, we believed that

5   The section draws from my article "Lay Elders Are Not the Shepherding JV Team," The Gospel Coalition (website), September 8, 2017, https://www.thegospelcoalition .org/article/lay-elders-are-not-shepherding-jv-team/.

a compensated clergy could be supported biblically and that this model resulted in a more efficient and connected elder team. We believed this was the most effective way to lead the church. I taught this. I wrote about it. And I staffed our local church according to this model. But something was missing.

Along the way I also helped churches where it seemed more effective and efficient to give power to a single preacher or leader who could articulate vision and direction. Sometimes this was a church planter who hadn't yet had the time or found the right people to form an elder team. At other times, it was a more congregational polity, where the church had one pastor and the deacons or elders served as little more than an advisory board.

In my journey, I've also helped leaders who served under or alongside pastors who were diabolically power-hungry. Popularly, these guys are known as the *fallen celebrity pastors*. Such men often pushed lay elders to the side to consolidate or enhance their own power and control.

Less insidious, but perhaps more dangerous, are cultures where a board of lay elders is in place, but its responsibility for holding the staff—and particularly the senior leader—accountable remains unarticulated and undefined.

Over the years, I've learned that the biblical model is different. This has been a key lesson in leadership development for me. Like Paul's ministry, our ministries should be marked by divestment, by self-forgetfulness. Our desire must be to see others develop their gifts and potentialities. We must push the power out—giving away our resources, influence, talents, and authority to other leaders. And one way to apply this is by appointing and empowering nonvocational elders. I think it's still important for some elders to be compensated for their work (1 Tim. 5:17). But I've come to believe that a great way to spread out power is to ensure that some are not. Here are four reasons why.

First, lay elders provide wider protection. On this fallen planet, money impacts every environment it touches. When a governing body is composed exclusively of men whose financial future is tied to the organization, this can tempt them toward expedience, and it can render them less circumspect with certain important decisions. It may seem noble, but it's still naive to manage a staff while assuming that humility or long relationships can overrule the influence of these economic and political dynamics.

Non-staff elders look through a lens that's less clouded by how decisions affect next year's budget or next week's attendance. Lay elders aren't godlier or supernaturally impervious to income and attendance stats. It's just that they don't work for the church, so their decisions are less likely to be influenced by them. They're unencumbered by the way their leadership impacts salary or standing within the church. In this way, lay elders are uniquely positioned to protect the interests of the church as well as any staff members who come under unexpected criticism.

I know a pastor whose first wife rushed headlong into a wall of egregious sins without repentance. Though the pastor was cleared by his elder team—most of them nonvocational—the congregation was scandalized by the subsequent divorce, and the people voted with their feet. Membership dropped, income plummeted, and the church ran aground on the shores of chaos. The pastor offered to resign, but the elders believed he was called to preach. So, despite the Monday-morning stats, they felt the

ACKNOWLEDGING AND SHARING POWER

Lay elders aren't godlier or supernaturally impervious to income and attendance stats. It's just that they don't work for the church, so their decisions are less likely to be influenced by them.

church's future was best secured through protecting his role. They strengthened him through their prayers and encouragement, and they called him to stay leashed to the mast until the church came through the storm.

That was many years ago. This pastor is now happily remarried, and the church has bounced back with strength. I recently asked if he thought he'd still be pastoring his church if all of the elders were vocational and under the squeeze of a rapid decline in attendance and giving. "Probably not," he said. Then he observed, "When a congregation raises serious questions about a staff member and an unpopular decision needs to be made, it's a comfort to know that there are elders in the room whose job and economic future aren't tied to the way they vote." I think he was right.

Second, lay elders provide stability and a stronger investment. In some Christian traditions, pastoral ministry is seen as both a calling and a career path. This means that men will spend a few years pastoring in one place and then move up the ranks to a larger church. The practice isn't all wrong; it's good to invest in younger men and give them greater influence as they grow in wisdom. But the ambitious drives of a career mindset can easily corrupt the soul of ministry. And when leadership roles are all a revolving door, this can destabilize the local church.

Nonvocational elders don't have these temptations. They aren't building their lives around paid ministry, so they can be deeply invested. Even though paid elders may move on, lay elders remain. And when they stand their post, they serve as custodians of history and the rich gospel story that sounds forth from their church. Certainly, there are situations where rigid elders have protected dead traditions. But in a healthy church it's more likely that their experience, long-term relationships, and institutional knowledge smooth transitions and aid productive change.

Third, nonvocational elders provide deeper wisdom. It's simple economics. If all the elders are compensated, the elder team will be smaller. In this model the size of the plurality is determined by church finances, not church needs or eldership gifts. This can mean the river of wisdom runs narrow and hazardously shallow. But an "abundance of counselors" provides a safer passage (Prov. 11:14).

"Abundance" is admittedly an abstract term. It doesn't prescribe an ideal size for your plurality, but it does suggest a number that is beyond what you can compensate. Most churches across the globe are small. When we make the role of elder contingent on the church's budget rather than the number of qualified men who aspire, we can create a model where the only churches that can enjoy an abundance of elders are Western and affluent.

For those who may argue that it's too much to call a layperson to the rigors of elder training and assessment, I answer with these words from Alexander Strauch:

> Some people say, "You can't expect laymen to raise their families, work all day, and shepherd a local church." But that is simply

not true. Many people raise families, work, and give substantial hours of time to community service, clubs, athletic activities, and/or religious institutions. The cults have built up large lay movements that survive primarily because of the volunteer time of their members. We Bible-believing Christians are becoming a lazy, soft, pay-for-it-to-be-done group of Christians. It is positively amazing how much people can accomplish when they are motivated to work for something they love. I've seen people build and remodel houses in their spare time. I've also seen men discipline themselves to gain a phenomenal knowledge of the Scriptures.

The real problem then lies not in men's limited time and energy but in false ideas about work, Christian living, life's priorities and—especially—Christian ministry.[6]

Finally, non-staff elders provide a broader take on issues. The vantage point of lay elders is unique, so they provide a unique perspective. They bring a marketplace and civilian perspective to our church leadership discussions. It's distinct and, I would argue, necessary for certain strategic decisions. A church is not simply a community and a cause but also a corporation.[7] If you want the mission to succeed, you need the organization to support it.

Pastors tend to be wired for community and cause. But the corporation part—with all its graphs and policies—is often assumed or ignored. Businessmen, on the other hand, traffic every day

---

6 Alexander Strauch, *Biblical Eldership: An Urgent Call to Restore Biblical Church Leadership* (Littleton, CO: Lewis and Roth, 1995), 28.

7 I'm grateful to Jim Dethmer for his conception of the church existing within the tensions of community, cause, and corporation.

> *A church is not simply a community and a cause but also a corporation. If you want the mission to succeed, you need the organization to support it.*

in a world that understands the connections between organization and mission. When such men are also qualified elders, their take can supply the eldership with advice that is both missionally strategic and biblically shrewd (Matt. 10:16).

There's something else too.

Paid pastors often get the polished sides of people. Postmodernity may be in full bloom, but people still think twice before dropping profanity in the presence of a staff pastor. Lay elders, by contrast, aren't met with the same filters and forced spirituality. The congregation perceives non-staff guys as more *us* than *them*.

It's not that the lay elders are more humble or accessible than the guys on the payroll. The gulf between paid clergy and laity has never been merely an organizational problem. It's a divide that runs right through the human heart. The presence of nonvocational men in the eldership acknowledges this reality and wisely seeks to bridge the gap.

It's also not about converting the church into a mini-republic to ensure that there is congregational representation within the eldership. I think it's more about church identification by the eldership. Lay elders can easily identify with the triumphs and temptations, the wisdom and weakness that visit church members from nine to five each day. By yoking lay elders with paid pastors, the eldership can better know the condition of their flocks and pay careful attention to them (Prov. 27:23; Acts 20:28).

Empowering Every Leader

Nonvocational elders are hardly some magical key that will unlock all the polity perplexities that dog evangelicals. Every leadership model has its kryptonite. But empowering lay elders does acknowledge and demonstrate the truth that even those who have been given great power have limits. If our churches are led by paid staff alone, we're missing out on essential gifts. The combination of broader wisdom, deeper insight into the marketplace, unique perspectives on church health, and freedom from economic concerns is absolutely vital. Here's why: if we're going to steward power well, we must share it and steward it together.

The more the apostle gave away his power, the more influence he gained. That's because when power is shared, it's not lost; it's multiplied!

Jonathan Leeman, of the ministry 9Marks, once wrote a helpful article entitled "How Mark Dever Passes Out Authority."[8] Leeman described how Pastor Dever is rather constantly confronted with the opportunity to accrue authority, but he gives most of it away. Dever builds the ministry with his elder team first. He limits his preaching slots to 50–60 percent of the time. He lets others steal his ideas. He speaks sparingly at elder meetings; he doesn't even chair them. He invites criticism from members of the congregation. Leeman spends the second half of the article

---

8   Jonathan Leeman, "How Mark Dever Passes Out Authority," The Gospel Coalition (website), January 16, 2014, https://www.thegospelcoalition.org/article/how-mark -dever-passes-out-authority/.

describing how this leadership model has profoundly influenced the culture of Dever's local church. Chief among these are the ways this culture destroys natural social hierarchies and cultivates a willingness to forgive.

As I read this article, it occurred to me that Dever's self-emptying has impacted his church to such a degree that he is actually valued more. In other words, the fears that lie behind our reticence to give away power—*I'll be forgotten; I'll be taken advantage of; I'll become useless*—wither like weeds under the heat of gospel truth. You see, when Christ emptied himself of power, he was exalted (Phil. 2:6–9). The same was true for Paul. The more the apostle gave away his power, the more influence he gained. That's because when power is shared, it's not lost; it's multiplied![9]

We must push down power to achieve a greater prize. This takes courage and a clarity that is fueled by faith. That's what I want for you; that's what I want for me. Most importantly, that's what I believe God wants for his church.

---

9 Gordon Smith writes: "Shared power does not mean diffused power. It does not mean that power is diminished. Shared power results in more power. The organization is more powerful, more effective and more capable of fulfilling its mission as those within the organization recognize and affirm the legitimate exercise of power and appreciate the diverse ways it is expressed within the institution." *Institutional Intelligence: How to Build Effective Organizations* (Downers Grove, IL: InterVarsity Press, 2017), 57.

7

The Plurality Tune-Up

ELDER PLURALITIES ARE both delicate and durable.[1] On the one hand, an elder team provides the local church with strength, bearing the weight of leading the church forward against all odds. Just ponder Christian history: healthy pluralities have stood defiantly against antagonistic cultures, hostile governments, sin, and the devil himself.

At the same time, it must be said that it's easy for a plurality to fall apart. There's always the danger that the elders will run aground over some knotty issue. They can lose sight of the most important things and end up focusing on peripheral issues. The margins become the main thing. Discernment is lost. Leaders lose the plot.

A plurality doesn't run on a set-it-and-forget-it recipe. An elder team is like delicate, powerful machinery that needs regular inspection and maintenance in order to remain healthy.

---

1   This chapter draws from my articles "The Plurality Dashboard" (parts 1 and 2), Rev Dave Harvey (website), March 29, 2016, https://revdaveharvey.com/2016/03/29/plurality-dashboard-part-one/; and April 30, 2016, https://revdaveharvey.com/2016/04/30/plurality-dashboard-part-two/.

So how do we know if a plurality is healthy? A healthy elder team must be more than the names that appear in the incorporating documents or that show up under the "elders" tab on the church website. Whenever two or more men are gathered, some sort of culture emerges. The only question is whether or not that culture is healthy, or at least heading toward health.

As the elders go, so goes the church.

Eldership and leadership are incarnational. Our convictions take on flesh. Healthy pluralities must embody common values, mutual respect, collaborative relationships, and a sense of their shared history and responsibilities. Embodying this sort of culture takes time and effort; a plurality does not magically become a band of brothers. But the effort is worth it. In fact, the importance of keeping the plurality cannot be overstated. Like it or not, the culture of an eldership determines the health of a church. As one popular pastor says, "Whatever the leaders are, the people become."[2]

This is not to diminish the role of the Holy Spirit, biblical preaching, mission, or any other means of grace that shape God's people. But without the agency of a healthy leadership team, these means can be quenched or curtailed. Simply put, *as the elders go, so goes the church.*

I've already given you an overview of what it takes to build a healthy plurality, and in the previous two chapters I talked about some of the mechanics necessary for maintaining the plurality. Now I'd like to give you a tool that will help you examine your

2   John MacArthur, "God's Standard for Leadership," Grace to You (blog), August 5, 2013, https://www.gty.org/library/blog/B130805/gods-standard-for-leadership/.

local elder team and keep it running together over the long haul. I like to use a four-cylinder engine as a metaphor—not because I was a gearhead growing up but because I think it's a solid analogy.

A cylinder is a giant tube in the engine within which the piston moves up and down to compress the gas and ignite the combustion. *If that doesn't sound right, blame Google; again, I'm the guy who feels triumphant because he can find the gas cap on his rental car . . . sometimes.* My point is that there are four factors—we'll call them *plurality cylinders*—that power the engine of our teams. When all these cylinders are firing, the team will accelerate the church forward on mission.

Inspecting the Plurality: The Four-Cylinder Engine

In Pennsylvania when I grew up, cars had to be inspected once each year. Inspections were always a hassle, but through the process of the inspection, the owner learned whether certain parts or systems in the car needed attention or replacement. This was a good process for new drivers, because they learned that inspecting the car is necessary to maintain it—both to keep you and others safe and to keep the car moving forward.

When all these cylinders are firing, the team will accelerate the church forward on mission.

Anyone joining an eldership team should have the same expectation. Starting with the four cylinders that I'm outlining below—agreement, trust, care, and fit—should help. We need to inspect these four cylinders regularly. Remember, finding a problem is not an indictment on the leadership or the quality of the church. Just as any car needs maintenance, teams do too. Where there are pluralities, there are inevitably problems. But the wise team minimizes these problems through regular inspection. Let's examine each plurality cylinder below and consider a few warning signs that could light up your dashboard.

The Agreement Cylinder: Are We on the Same Page?

Many well-intentioned—and faithful—men have sought to build a church around oversimplified belief statements such as "We believe in Jesus. Period." This approach serves neither the church, which looks to leaders for clarity, nor the elders, who live in confusion over what truly unites them. A plurality grounded in abstractions will never be a healthy team. When an elder team isn't clear about the basis of their unity, they'll find the agreement cylinder—and, as a result, the forward movement of the team— seizing up and breaking down in the face of major decisions.

Elders are called to define and protect the doctrinal borders of the church. The team doesn't need to agree on everything, but they do need to be united around essential doctrines, beginning with the gospel. The church is a theological entity. So, theological men united by theological agreement must lead it. This begins with a doctrinal unity grounded upon a statement of faith or common creeds and confessions to which each elder subscribes (Eph. 4:1–16). Here are some questions you can use to evaluate the scope of your theological unity:

- Do we agree on what is meant by the word *gospel* (1 Cor. 2:2–5; 15:1–8; Gal. 1:6–12)?
- Is the doctrinal basis of our unity as a team well defined?

- Do we have a statement of faith, and, if so, do we all affirm our statement of faith (Eph. 4:1–16)?
- Do we agree on the meaning of its terms (2 Tim. 2:14)?

Beyond our common confession, there's another part of the agreement cylinder. It's far subtler yet no less important. This is the matter of how well we work together as we talk through what we believe. Elderships become teams through timely, consistent, respectful, and vigorous theological discussion. Does your elder team employ care and wisdom when you discuss, debate, and differ on beliefs? Are you able to divide doctrines or discussions without dividing relationships? Here are some questions to monitor the quality of your theological conversations:

- Are we growing together theologically through study and discussion (2 Tim. 2:15)?
- When we disagree on less important doctrines or methodologies, do we do it wisely and with love (Eph. 4:1–3)?
- Is it clear to everyone that the elder team works hard to understand one another's positions and can represent them without exaggeration or misrepresentation (James 1:19)?

Some assume that disagreement or dissent will clog up the agreement cylinder. That common fallacy confuses dissent with disrespect or disloyalty. Humble elders who debate in ways that uphold the law of love actually improve the teamwork engine; they enhance the performance of the team.[3]

---

3   Jeffrey A. Sonnenfeld argues that a culture of open dissent is necessary for any leadership team to reach its potential and avoid the common dangers of groupthink. Sonnenfeld,

This doesn't always mean quiet debate. In his bestselling book *Outliers*, Malcolm Gladwell tells the story of a commercial aircraft that was headed for a crash. Wanting to avoid the collision, the plane's copilot and engineer both politely and deferentially suggested course changes to the captain. The more experienced captain readily dismissed the copilot's understated advice. And, because of the copilot's lack of urgency, the pilot never got the point. Minutes later, the aircraft splattered onto the side of a mountain.[4]

> *The team doesn't need to agree on everything, but they do need to be united around essential doctrines, beginning with the gospel.*

Strong elders value agreement, but they also know that hyper-deference comes with a steep cost. They know that mindless uniformity among the leadership weakens the church. They're able to see dashboard warning lights when there is undue deference to the loudest voice or a naive and misguided admiration of the lead pastor. And they're willing to speak.

The Trust Cylinder: Are We Honest and Humble with One Another?

Trust lies at the heart of a healthy plurality. Each man must be convinced of the sincerity and integrity of the other. If doubt is allowed to build up like dirt in an engine, the parts will become

---

"What Makes Great Boards Great," *Harvard Business Review*, September 2002, https://hbr.org/2002/09/what-makes-great-boards-great/.

4 Malcolm Gladwell, *Outliers: The Story of Success* (New York: Little, Brown and Company, 2008), 177–223.

corrosive and wear on each other, interfering with free and efficient operation. But when elders can speak honestly to the church, to one another, and to the lead pastor, this fosters a culture of honesty throughout the whole congregation, where each member feels free to voice concerns and be vulnerable about his or her weaknesses or temptations. Integrity deepens trust. Proverbs 10:9 says, "Whoever walks in integrity walks securely." Elders with integrity foster a culture of security.

Here are some questions that will help you to check the operation of the trust cylinder:

- Will you be loyal to God's word by being completely honest with me (Col. 1:28–29)?
- Will you judge me or exploit me when I show weakness (Luke 6:37)?
- Will you be patient with me in areas where I need to grow (1 Thess. 5:14)?
- Can you be discreet once you really know my temptations (Prov. 3:21)?
- Can I be confident you will not share what I confide to you with anyone who should not know?
- Do you have my back, but never for sin (Prov. 16:28)?

To achieve genuine loyalty, each elder must be confident of how each fellow team member will respond to the particulars of his fallenness. Serving as an elder situates each man on a perch with a good view into the lives of the other elders. You pray together, work together, think together, counsel together, rejoice together, assess together, and confess sins together. Sharing these experiences creates a clear view into the gifts, struggles, strengths, and weaknesses of the team. With this clear perspective, you stand armed with perspectives that can unite or divide, refine or weaken, build up or tear down. Your perspective gives you power in the lives of the other men, and how you handle that power will determine whether or not the other men trust you.

Serving as an elder situates each man on a perch with a good view into the lives of the other elders.

Recently I sat with a small group of men confessing their present struggles as well as their fears about the future. When I'm confident in their love for me—confident that they want my best—I'm more free to be vulnerable with them as well. I'm also better able to receive the compassion they express about my pain and their wise correction of my weakness and sin. Having this trust liberates me to speak freely to them in turn. Let's face it. Absent that kind of confidence, elders stay superficial, fearing that their temptations or weaknesses will become poker chips played against them in the future. Teams must cultivate loyalty, and loyalty says, "I will encourage your strengths without ignoring or exploiting your weaknesses."

This leads to a second check for the trust cylinder, the presence of humility. To move the plurality from a titular board to a working team, each man must believe that he needs the other men. He must experience and model Paul's analogy of the body (1 Cor. 12:12–27), where one assumes, *To grow, I need your help.* Inspecting the presence of humility can start with a few simple questions:

- Are you quick to listen or quick to speak (James 1:19)?

- Will you withdraw when there is misunderstanding (Matt. 5:23–24)?
- Will you be humble if I risk correcting you or sharing a weakness I see (Prov. 9:8)?

All Christian community tests our humility, but being part of a leadership team is like sitting for the bar exam; it's long, tricky, and absent of immediate results. You see, humility must be earned over time as individuals both suspect themselves first, not others, and serve others first, not themselves. With the passing of time, this sort of humility becomes a rich oil that helps the engine of loyalty run smoothly.

Honesty and humility will help you travel many treacherous roads. If you're in harsh conditions right now, remember that the beauty and simplicity of the plurality design illustrate the time-tested glory of the golden rule (Luke 6:31). As elders, we are simply agreeing to respond to life together in the same way we teach others to respond. And, amazingly, as we apply this teaching, trust and loyalty abound.

The Care Cylinder: Do We Encourage and Nurture One Another?

For a plurality to become a team, agreement and trust are essential. Yet the truth is that your elder team and church can't survive on those two cylinders alone. They'll carry you down the road for a few miles, but you'll eventually sputter out. Two more cylinders complete the engine: care and fit.

As we turn our inspection to the care cylinder, you're likely beginning to see how each of the cylinders is connected to the others. How can someone be cared for by those he neither agrees with nor trusts? The notion is unrealistic and naive. But when elders love, trust, and lock arms together, the channels of care open wide, and shepherds enjoy the blessing of being shepherded. According to Jesus, it's our love for one another, not our productivity and performance, that marks our discipleship (John 13:34–35).

What follows in these paragraphs is a review of material we covered in chapters 4 and 5, but it bears repeating. In a world where most anything can be outsourced and professionalized, it's easy for pastors to farm out their care. It's easy for them to find the primary help their souls need outside of the eldership, sometimes even outside the church. But care from an outside source shouldn't replace the more primary responsibility we have to care for the leaders within our own church community. A wise elder understands this principle. We can't preach that people should receive their primary shepherding care through their local church pastors and then exempt ourselves from the same care. As I said earlier, as the elders go, so goes the church; that is, the manner in which pastors receive care is the method and model they'll reinforce for their congregation.

We can't preach that people should receive their primary shepherding care through their local church pastors and then exempt ourselves from the same care.

But why would we outsource our care when God has given us what we need within the local body? God loves the men who shepherd his flock. He wants their souls to be nurtured and tended to. So he supplies sufficient grace to convert pluralities into love-filled teams. Here's a trustworthy principle: joy and delight come when we receive our primary care from a "neighbor who is near" (Prov. 27:10). When a team begins to experience that joy and delight, team identity begins to form. And when the team identity forms, the nurture and care of each member becomes even more important. Then the culture builds as each elder commits himself to providing care for the others.

Elders, here are some questions that may help you assess how well you are caring for one another:

- Is it clear to each of us that the state of his soul matters to the other elders as much as (or more than!) his performance (John 13:34–35)?
- Are our conversations more likely to be filled with encouragement or critique (Eph. 4:29)?
- Can we point to specific times—not merely once—when we talked about our lives, families, struggles, and temptations, that is, when we talked about something apart from ministry (James 5:16)?
- Does my feedback on your performance include encouragement (1 Thess. 5:11)?
- Does someone on this team know the temptations to which I am vulnerable (Gal. 6:2)?
- Would my wife feel free to call you if I were tanking? Why or why not?

The Fit Cylinder: Do We Enjoy Being with Each Other and Know Our Place on the Team?

A pastoral team that unites around their theological convictions, trusts one another, and models genuine love toward each other can work together in harmony. But there's one more thing essential for keeping the leadership engine running. In fact, this final cylinder, when overlooked, has the potential to shut down the other three.

Elders need to know that they fit. This means not just "fitting in" but knowing in their hearts and minds that they are called and gifted for the roles in which they are serving on the team. Tensions arise when a man desires a role for which he's not suited or in which he is not affirmed. Frustrations arise when a man desires a role that just isn't available. The truth is that a pastor may be a good fit on one team but not on another. A pastoral candidate whose personality or gifting does not mesh well with the team can dramatically shift the culture of the plurality and, indirectly, the entire church.

Fit is perhaps the most complicated cylinder to assess, but here are some questions to help you measure it. I've categorized them under three headings: endowment, expectations, and evaluation.

Endowment. We are hardwired as created beings with particular strengths, talents, and proclivities. We're uniquely gifted. When we explore the path of our endowments, we'll find the kinds of ministry, roles, and people with which we best fit. Understanding how you've been gifted will lead you to that place where your labors will bear the greatest fruit.

Here are some questions to evaluate endowment:

- How well do we understand the gifts God has given each of us, and how well are our responsibilities aligned with those gifts (Rom. 12:6)?
- Though each elder is distinct, does my personality appear to mesh well with these men?

- Are we able to work together in ways that deepen our relationships rather than strain them?
- Does our time together (or with a potential elder) incite greater joy and creativity in our roles, or does it yield frustration and discouragement?

Expectations. It's not only important to know your gifts and endowments. It's also essential for healthy pluralities that expectations be defined—that there be clarity about the hopes and expectations for particular roles. Questions to ask could include these:

- Do I know my role and what is expected of me (Acts 6:1–7)?
- Do I have a written job description?
- Do I know to whom I report?
- How should I communicate to my co-laborers and the elder in charge of this area?
- Is my commitment to serve the church thorough enough to support a change of roles (Mark 10:45)?

Clarifying expectations requires each elder—particularly staff elders—to dispense of any faux spirituality that resists clear definition of a role or ministry. We must always be open, clear, and bold with our expectations. As servants of Christ committed to the best for his church, we realize that sometimes our expectations or roles need to change to best serve the church. But that doesn't eliminate the need for clear expectations.

This important principle is as old as the New Testament church. In Acts 6, each widow had the apostles' attention daily. It was a beautiful, organic, relational picture of community, and it was a wonderful phase of ministry for the Jerusalem church. But the church matured. As the church grew, the organism had to organize, and this meant that the apostles' roles needed to change. The delivery of care to the widows would come through different hands as the apostles needed to give their attention to more strategic service, namely, "to prayer and to the ministry of the word" (Acts 6:4).

Maturing expectations and the effect of changing expectations on a leader's fit matters. Each day the apostles served in a particular and perhaps predictable way. They were among the people, serving those with desperate needs. The expectations were clear. But as the church began to grow, their roles and expectations had to change. Sometimes it is for the better when we move on to duties we enjoy more. At other times moving on means emptying ourselves and taking the lower seat (Luke 14:10; Phil. 2:5–11).

Organizational discipline and adaptation are important for any church moving toward health.

For the Jerusalem church, the result was even greater fruit as "the word of God continued to increase, and the number of the disciples multiplied greatly in Jerusalem, and a great many of the priests became obedient to the faith" (Acts 6:7).

Here's the point. When the Jerusalem church leaders found their fit and defined the expectations, that led to a healthier church and a people more satisfied in their service. What do we learn? Organizational discipline and adaptation are important for any church moving toward health.

Evaluation. The last part of fit is evaluation. To arrive at different roles, the leaders of the Jerusalem church had to engage in

132

some touchy, seemingly dispassionate examination. Should the roles of those serving the widows be changed? This question was dangerous. Widows were among the most vulnerable people in the land. God himself joins the discussion when the care of widows is evaluated (Ps. 68:5; Jer. 49:11; James 1:27). Nevertheless, these leaders engaged in a difficult assessment of their roles, their daily to-do lists, their responsibilities, and their gifts. From this Spirit-led evaluation came fruit and growth.

When one reads the requirements for elders or deacons, it's clear that *evaluation* is a doorway to ministry. When Paul tells Timothy, "Keep a close watch on yourself and on the teaching" (1 Tim. 4:16), it's clear that evaluation doesn't end at the front door.

Here are some questions to help elderships gauge the place evaluation currently plays within their cultures:

- Have we clearly defined how we will evaluate one another and what determines success?
- Am I, in particular, aware of the specific contexts where we will regularly evaluate our fruitfulness as a team?
- Have we clarified the process by which each of us can share concerns about how he is being handled or assessed (Titus 1:6–9)?

Central to the matter of fit (and to all the cylinders for that matter!) is the gospel, with its God-preeminent, church-loving, and flesh-killing claims. A healthy elder team won't happen overnight. You won't walk into the perfect situation, and you won't luck into it. Furthermore, it'll take hard work and dedication to keep it running, once you enjoy health. You'll have to crucify your pride, push down your fears, and hold on to the promises. But in the end, the fruit is sweet. When the gospel works gloriously into your team dynamics, it will also affect the hearts of your congregation.

Finishing Strong

The goal of a plurality is not just starting strong. We want our churches to be missional and see God move in powerful ways. But, no less, we want to finish the race. That's part of the reason why we're bound together in this brotherhood. We want this church to finish with strength. The goal is not just starting strong; it's not growing fast; it's remaining together. That's why Paul's words in Philippians 1:3–6 are so captivating:

> I thank my God in all my remembrance of you, always in every prayer of mine for you all making my prayer with joy, because of your partnership in the gospel from the first day until now. And I am sure of this, that he who began a good work in you will bring it to completion at the day of Jesus Christ.

What a great vision of what a plurality should look like. It's a long-haul vision. It's worth the time and energy it takes to keep the four cylinders running smoothly. My prayer is that as you tend to each cylinder, they all will power the engine of a maturing plurality for your church. Why? Because the quality of your plurality determines the health of your church!

8

The Joy-Boosting Delight
of Shared Ministry

IN HIS BOOK *Tribe: On Homecoming and Belonging*, Sebastian Junger explores a fascinating phenomenon that unfolded during the time of the early New World settlements—an anomaly rarely mentioned in American history books. Some of the early European settlers defected from their colonial camps to live among the Native Americans. In the public schools I attended, I never heard *that*. But apparently the settlers saw among the native tribes a thriving embodiment of community, camaraderie, and unity. Then, when they looked around their own neighborhoods, they felt that the New World was missing some good old qualities—things like companionship and solidarity. The loss was too painful, the ache too severe; so, dramatic action was needed. Junger describes the results:

> The intensely *communal* nature of an Indian tribe held an appeal that the *material* benefits of Western civilization couldn't necessarily compete with. . . . As early as 1612, Spanish authorities noted in amazement that forty or fifty Virginians had married into Indian tribes, and that even English women were

openly mingling with the natives. At that point, whites had been in Virginia for only a few years, and many who joined the Indians would have been born and raised in England. These were not rough frontiersmen who were sneaking off to join the savages; these were the sons and daughters of Europe.[1]

Junger goes on to explain how the European settlements would send delegations to take back the defectors, but the attempts mostly failed. No one wanted to return. When the colonists went to rescue their people from a Native American tribe, the defectors were determined to stay. No rescue was necessary. They had found a home, and they were willing to make sacrifices to remain there. Community meant more to them than the comforts of their former way of life.

When a plurality's partnership is strong, joy in ministry runs deep.

As we have journeyed together through this book, we've discovered that *plurality* is a weighty word. I've tried to persuade you that New Testament leadership was a team enterprise, not one man's genius. Thus, when leaders acted, it was *together* as a ruling *body* (Acts 13:1–3; 15:22–23). Taking it one step further, I've argued that a quality plurality is essential for a healthy church; that is to say, when elders share their leadership and life together, the church thrives. This point is so important that I provided a method for evaluating the health of your plurality in chapter 7.

---

1 Sebastian Junger, *Tribe: On Homecoming and Belonging* (New York: Twelve Hachette, 2016), 10.

Before you reach this book's conclusion, I want to offer one final truth about plurality. It's the beautiful experience those European settlers pursued when they defected from their individualistic communities to live with the Native American tribes. *When a plurality's partnership is strong, joy in ministry runs deep.*

The Twin Marks of Joyful Plurality

Church planters have the opportunity to build and develop a plurality of elders through a slow and measured process. It's not effortless, mind you, but these men have time on their side. And the eldership manuals by Strauch, Dever, or Bannerman are companions to guide them along the way.[2]

Others, like me in my first pastorate, inherit a plurality almost overnight through a church crisis, or perhaps through being hired to lead an established church. Right away, one discovers that having a plurality of elders is not synonymous with enjoying a united leadership team. Surprisingly, shared values, mutual respect, relational history, denominational affiliation, and constitutional responsibility do not automatically conjure up the kind of culture where doing ministry together is joyful.

In fact, church cultures are sometimes marked by rivalry, self-protection, and competing agendas. The apostle Paul got this.

---

2   Alexander Strauch, *Biblical Eldership: An Urgent Call to Restore Biblical Church Leadership* (Littleton, CO: Lewis and Roth, 1995); Robert M. Thune, *Gospel Eldership: Equipping a New Generation of Servant Leaders* (Greensboro, NC: New Growth, 2016); see also Mark Dever, ed., *Polity: Biblical Arguments on How to Conduct Church Life* (Washington, DC: Center for Church Reform, 2001); James Bannerman, *The Church of Christ* (Carlisle, PA: Banner of Truth, 2015); and Timothy Paul Jones and Michael S. Wilder, *The God Who Goes before You: Pastoral Leadership as Christ-Centered Followership* (Nashville: B&H Academic, 2018).

While the Philippian church and its leadership had many assets, wholehearted unity was not among them. Paul exhorts the church, "Do nothing from selfish ambition or conceit, but in humility count others more significant than yourselves" (Phil. 2:3). Selfish ambition and conceit were undermining the unity and joy in the Philippian church. Later on, in chapter 4, Paul mentions two women, Euodia and Syntyche, with disagreement so pronounced that he must address it publicly—from prison!

The greater the unity among the workers, the deeper their joy in the work.

This wasn't just messy for Paul; it was joy-killing. For him, unity inspired delight. "Complete my joy by being of the same mind, having the same love, being in full accord and of one mind" (Phil. 2:2). When we dissect Paul's vision of unity, we find gritty ingredients like humility (Phil. 2:3) and an earnest commitment to the interests of others (Phil. 2:4). When these key values are practiced, team cultures grow healthy, and ministry becomes sweet.

Paul's vision reminds us of a principle that's true of pluralities: *The greater the unity among the workers, the deeper their joy in the work.* Allow me to unpack this a little more. What's the connection between a healthy leadership community and delight in ministry? And what is it about the marks of humble surrender and commitment that deliver us joy?

The Joy in Surrendering

In his book *Leaders Eat Last*, Simon Sinek tells the story of a former undersecretary of defense who gave a speech at a large conference. The decorated official took his place on the stage and began his speech. Then he paused to take a sip of coffee from the Styrofoam cup that he'd brought with him on stage. Sinek describes the scene:

He took another sip, looked down at the cup and smiled.

"You know," he said, interrupting his own speech, "I spoke here last year. I presented at this same conference on this same stage. But last year, I was still an undersecretary," he said. "I flew here in business class and when I landed, there was someone waiting for me at the airport to take me to my hotel. Upon arriving at my hotel," he continued, "there was someone else waiting for me. They had already checked me into the hotel, so they handed me my key and escorted me up to my room. The next morning, when I came down, again there was someone waiting for me in the lobby to drive me to this same venue that we are in today. I was taken through a back entrance, shown to the green room and handed a cup of coffee in a beautiful ceramic cup."

"But this year, as I stand here to speak to you, I am no longer the undersecretary," he continued. "I flew here coach class and when I arrived at the airport yesterday there was no one there to meet me. I took a taxi to the hotel, and when I got there, I checked myself in and went by myself to my room. This morning, I came down to the lobby and caught another taxi to come here. I came in the front door and found my way backstage. Once there, I asked one of the techs if there was any coffee. He pointed to a coffee machine on a table against the wall. So I walked over and poured myself a cup of coffee into this here Styrofoam cup," he said as he raised the cup to show the audience.

"It occurs to me," he continued, "the ceramic cup they gave me last year . . . it was never meant for me at all. It was meant for the position I held. I deserve a Styrofoam cup."[3]

The truth is that we all deserve the Styrofoam cup. There are undeniable perks and advantages that come with being a pastor or elder in a local church. But they aren't meant for us as individuals. They're meant for the role we fill. As roles change, privileges must be transferred. Guys who don't get this often tank after transitions.

Only Jesus has an unalterable role. The rest of us are just keeping the seat warm for the next guy. The day will come when we will vacate our roles and surrender our privileges to the ones who come behind us. When that day comes for you, remember to give up the beautiful ceramic mug and embrace the Styrofoam cup.

In Philippians, Paul makes clear that the path to joyful partnership runs through surrender. He writes. "Do nothing from selfish ambition or conceit, but in humility count others more significant than yourselves" (Phil. 2:3). Effective teams aren't built when elders constantly assert their rights or indulge self-exalting dreams for glory. Rather, unity comes when we surrender our claims of significance and count one another better than ourselves. When humble character inspires an unselfish culture, healthy teams are formed and sustained. When describing Lincoln's team of rivals, Doris Kearns Goodwin offered a very insightful one-liner: "In his paradigm of team leadership, greatness was grounded in

3   Simon Sinek, *Leaders Eat Last* (New York: Penguin, 2017), 84–85.

goodness."[4] One might wonder whether old Abe lifted that approach straight out of Philippians 2!

"Have this mind among yourselves, which is yours in Christ Jesus, who, though he was in the form of God, did not count equality with God a thing to be grasped, but emptied himself, by taking the form of a servant" (Phil. 2:5–7). Jesus could have kept the privileges of heaven, but he knew there was a greater joy in surrendering them. For the sake of that joy, Jesus endured the cross (Phil. 2:8–11; Heb. 12:1–2). What's amazing is that Jesus is the only man in human history who truly deserved all of his privileges. And yet he found joy in renouncing certain prerogatives—in becoming like us to make us more like him. He was delighted to make us partakers of his glory. Jesus found joy in humbly spreading those privileges around.

Paul makes clear that the path to joyful partnership runs through surrender.

Because he loved us in this way, we can follow his path. We too can surrender.

The Joy in Commitment

When Paul wrote the elders and deacons in Philippi, he didn't just want them to be humble and unified for the value of their own joy. Nor did he address this group as a set of ministry professionals who would dutifully mobilize for mission. When Paul gave joyful

4   Doris Kearns Goodwin, *Team of Rivals: The Political Genius of Abraham Lincoln* (New York: Simon & Schuster, 2006), 226.

thanks for their "partnership [*koinōnia*] in the gospel from the first day until now" (Phil. 1:5), he was writing to leaders whom he knew well and loved dearly, leaders to whom he felt devoted.

When love makes a promise, real commitments—the durable kind—are born.

Paul's idea of a *koinōnia*, a partnering fellowship, included an intentional commitment to the Philippians' welfare. The apostle's ongoing connection with the Philippian church was one of nourishment and strengthening. That's why he deploys Timothy and Epaphroditus in Philippians 2:19–30. His goal for the Philippians wasn't transactional—you scratch my back, I'll scratch yours. No, he was committed to them (v. 20). He wanted this church to be encouraged, to be joyfully cheered up by the ministry they'd receive from the visiting friends he was sending back to them (vv. 19, 28). He was seeking the fruit that increases to their credit (Phil 4:18).

You see, when love makes a promise, real commitments—the durable kind—are born. When those commitments are directed toward others, particularly within a team of leaders, it raises us above our own maladies and absurdities to opportunities provided by the mission and the needs of others. In short, our common commitments bring us joy. It was true in Philippi, and has been proven true throughout history.

What's Your Vision?

Do you remember my story about the European settlers who joined the Native American tribes? Attempts to rescue them were unnecessary because the fleeing settlers had found a new home among the native peoples. Their new community was a place where radical individualism and corrupted ambition were unwelcome. Why? Because those tribes were willing to commit themselves to the glorious idea of a connected and committed community. And while they did not exalt Christ, common grace allowed them to exhibit tribal partnership, one that seemed superior to the lifeless communities from which the settlers had fled.

Here's what I'm trying to say: truly shared, truly collaborative ministry is worth it.

When our pluralities see the beauty of a committed and humble unity and then make the sacrifices necessary to have our teams embody it, we'll flourish. When we recognize that the true tendons that tie leaders together are not the polity particulars but the system of trusting relationships among the participants, we'll thrive.

> *When our pluralities see the beauty of a committed and humble unity and then make the sacrifices necessary to have our teams embody it, we'll flourish.*

No polity, no matter how biblical, can withstand a lack of trust. Yes, without exception, elders must have creedal commitments. But the real glue, the supreme stickiness that makes us durable—that makes it worth it—is in the grit of our mercy, goodness, integrity, Christlike character, and reciprocal love. It is greatness grounded in goodness. Without humility, churches—both older congregations and exciting young ones that are growing quickly on the charisma of one leader—will become monuments within one generation.

You see, a plurality is not merely a *collection* of autonomous leaders. It's more importantly a group of *connected* elders, growing together within an ecosystem where they can flourish. For pluralities to last, ministry must be shared; commitment must be collaborative.

In the best eldership, life is a shared experience. While there must be order and leadership, healthy churches do not display the hierarchies of autocracy. Rather, they emerge as a dynamic movement of leaders synchronized by doctrine and relationships to achieve together what no single leader can accomplish alone. These relational and convictional connections stir a different set of expectations for the plurality. It's not that there is no place for obligations, rights, and expectations. But the trust engendered from mutual care and connection stirs more-noble desires, such as the longing to be known, the desire to contribute to a greater cause, the yearning to give and care, and the call to build something together that will serve the next generation. These dynamic connections change the key organizational questions from "What do I get?" to "To whom do I belong, and what claim does this make upon my life?"

> *For pluralities to last, ministry must be shared; commitment must be collaborative.*

Not long ago, *Christianity Today* commemorated the passing of the remarkable Billy Graham. One article commented on Graham's commitment to minister through a team:

> I learned from Graham to build your ministry on a team. He knew this, and he built a core team that was with him 50 years.

Everybody on the team brought strengths to the table. When you build an effective team, you hire people who compensate for your weaknesses and who mobilize or reinforce your strengths, because nobody can be good at everything.[5]

The great evangelist understood something. Good teams make us better. I'm talking not about moral improvement but about the kind of culture that calls us to a manner of life that is worthy of the gospel (Phil. 1:27). Our plurality is not a place for consumers or for those who crave distinction through a platform; such motivation tears at the social fabric that binds us together. Maybe a better way to say it is this: good teams bring God greater glory.

Better Together!

You get the heart of this book, don't you? Think about it: We all cherish our memories of having accomplished something with a group of people that made us better. Maybe you won a big game, fixed an intractable problem, addressed an injustice, united to plant a church or to build a new facility. These are the sorts of moments when we feel alive. They're the times when we experienced our gifts being used in the service of a higher ideal. *I* faded into the background, and *we* won the day. Now, you can look back and remember that moment of flourishing. And you know, deep down inside, that there is an intrinsic value to interdependence that can never be replaced by something else.

Together we sense that we should give our lives to this biblical

---

5 Rick Warren, "Rick Warren: What I Learned from Billy," *Christianity Today*, April 2018, 36.

ideal, even though it may cost us dearly, or even scar us deeply. We grasp that the true heroes of the future are the ones who may have been sinned against by the institutions they love, but they still fight for those institutions' existence and sacrifice for their future. True heroes understand that we are better together.

And so we take the risk and live devoted to this biblical vision of plurality, not because we have perfect communion—we're still fallen and flawed—but because we know deep in the recesses of our souls that the only leadership story worth living is a life where we lead together. As we commit to one another, we cultivate the courage to love boldly, suffer graciously, build with longevity, and trust God unshakably. And, in our humble, other-centered commitment to one another, churches are built and people are served. In this exhilarating and sacrificial culture where self goes to die, we find resilience; we discover camaraderie; we experience the unexpected joy of serving the Savior who died for us that we might lead like him!

Appendix 1

Elders, Care for Your Senior Pastor

THE PHONE CALL just ended.[1] It was a wonderful hour spent talking with the lead pastor of a thriving metropolitan church. He indicated that his next few days included a sermon to prepare, a funeral, the residual cleanup involved in acquiring a building, dozens of decisions for the church, guarding his heart as someone who had been sinned against, tending to his growing family, and, well, you get the point.

This dude was spent and being spent.

"Who cares for your soul?" I asked. He spoke lovingly of his elders but honestly recognized that none of them, himself included, had been equipped to care for each other. Each elder had been trained within a now-defunct megachurch that emphasized productivity over people and numerical growth over personal care.

It's a story I hear all too often in my travels. Those who are called to care receive little of it themselves. But surprisingly, and by the grace of God, it was not my experience as a senior pastor.

---

1   This appendix builds on my article "Caring for Your Lead (and Campus!) Pastor," Rev Dave Harvey (website), July 31, 2015, https://revdaveharvey.com/2015/07/31/caring-for-your-lead-and-campus-pastor/.

By the grace of God, I've been the object of care from many godly men, guys who knew well how to effectively nurture the leader's soul.

Here are some things I learned from being the object of wise care.

Care Has Legs

A lead pastor lives a busy, frenetic life. That's not a critique; it's usually necessary if he is going to fulfill the job description of being first among equals for a people who are themselves busy, mobile, and digitally connected.

It takes initiative for meaningful care to hit that kind of moving target. Initiative gives care legs to run on. Well-aimed and intentional care of a lead or senior pastor means knowing his burdens. No rocket science here; you can't help carry a burden that you don't know exists. Taking initiative is what connects your desire to serve with his need for care. Proverbs 20:5 says,

> The purpose in a man's heart is like deep water,
> but a man of understanding will draw it out.

This means that if you want to know what's swimming in the deep water of your lead pastor's heart, you've got to take initiative and drop the bucket in.

I've had team members who knew how to lower the bucket into my heart. As I write this, faces flash before me with names like Andy, Orlando, Mark, and Josh. These guys would ask: "How's your soul? Where is the gospel real to you right now? How is Kimm doing? Where are you being tempted?" They might pose these questions during spontaneous visits to my office. Theirs was a constant stream of care flowing from a heart of loving initiative.

Initiative includes prayer. Elders, do you pray for your senior leader? If so, are your prayers informed by his actual struggles because you've dropped the bucket in and taken the initiative to ask? I know men have prayed for me. I know because they tell me, which becomes a heartening thing to hear for an embattled soul. Others have sent passages to encourage me or focus my own meditation. Every contact, call, or text became a reminder that I was not alone, that there was someone who understood the deep waters I was treading and who was helping me stay afloat (see chart A.1).

Chart A.1. Care has legs

Elders, provide a constant stream of care for your pastor flowing from a heart of loving initiative.

> *The purpose in a man's heart is like deep water,*
>> *but a man of understanding will draw it out. (Prov. 20:5)*

Care Initiates
- How is your soul?
- Where is the gospel real to you right now?
- Are you connecting well with your wife and kids this week?
- Where are you being tempted?

Care Prays
- Am I praying for my pastor?
- Does my pastor know and feel that his church is truly praying for him?
- Are my prayers informed by his actual struggles because I've cared enough to take the initiative to ask?
- What passages could I send to my pastor that might encourage him?

Care Has Teeth

Lead pastors live in the tension between two huge priorities: the home and the church. John Piper calls it "pastoral polygamy," saying: "Now this is something to wonder at. Two deep commitments of my life—each wanting more of my time, more of my love, more of my energy, and more of my creativity—but each sticking up for the other and pleading the cause of the other and caring about the other."[2] A wise pastor like Piper understands the priority of his marriage and family, but he is using the analogy of polygamy to identify a reality that anyone caring for a lead guy must understand: the delicate balance of priorities along with the need for accountability.

Elders, your senior leader needs your help in protecting his priorities. Sabbath, date nights, sufficient vacation time, exercise, special times with his kids—all of this is your business if you're serious about caring for your lead pastor. You may know these are priorities for him, because he preaches about rest regularly. But sometimes the needs of the church distract him from applying his doctrine of rest as well as he preaches it. No worries—God gave him *you*, the elders around him, to serve his soul by advocating for his family. And if he is the rare leader who struggles with laziness, perhaps you need to advocate for the church too!

Elders, who has been appointed to know the state of your senior pastor's marriage? Who ensures that he's getting time off and not sliding into his mental office on his Sabbath? Who looks into

2   John Piper, "Reflections on 25 Years of Marriage and the Wonders of Pastoral 'Polygamy,'" Desiring God (website), December 15, 2019, https://www.desiringgod.org/articles/reflections-on-25-years-of-marriage-and-the-wonders-of-pastoral-polygamy.

whether he's *getting real* in his small group? Who's asking about his Internet use or his struggles with parenting? Who represents the elders in graciously saying, "Baloney!" if the man leading your congregation is deceiving himself?

Who gives his care teeth?

Every eldership should know exactly who provides the practical care and accountability for the lead pastor and should live with confidence that this group of people is doing its job well (see chart A.2).

Chart A.2. Care has teeth

Elders, care for your pastor by protecting his priorities and advocating for his family.

An overseer must be above reproach, the husband of one wife. . . .
He must manage his own household well. (1 Tim. 3:2, 4)

Care Protects

- Who knows the state of your pastor's marriage?
- Who ensures he's getting time off and faithfully resting?
- Who looks into whether he's getting real in his relationships?
- Who asks about Internet use or struggles with marriage and parenting?

Care Advocates

- How can you encourage him in his home life?
- Where can you step in to serve his entire family?
- When could you begin implementing a pastoral sabbatical?
- How can you actively create a culture of support for your pastor and his family?

Care Means Open Hands

Unless your church is confused or unhealthy, your senior pastor is in his role because he is uniquely gifted in ways that really help the church. This probably has something to do with preaching, leadership, and shepherding. Elders, your job is to make sure he is dedicating himself to those things. This won't happen unless you open your hands to release him.

Releasing someone to live out of his gifts is an attitude before it's an action. It means you see your role as making him effective. As we've discussed, that happens when elders count others more significant than themselves (Phil. 2:3) and look not only to their own interests but also to the interests of the others (Phil. 2:4). When teams embrace the gospel, those who are coequal subordinate themselves to another for the good of the mission.

The executive pastor of the church I led was exceptional at this. Mark would often ask me what he could take off my plate. He seemed particularly pleased when he could help me to be more strategic and productive. To Mark, this role was not a stepping stone. It was the place where he was called to make others a success (see chart A.3).

Chart A.3. Care means open hands

Elders, care for your pastor by freeing him to dedicate himself to the use of his God-given gifts.

In humility count others more significant than yourselves. Let each of you look not only to his own interests, but also to the interests of others. (Phil. 2:3–4)

Care Serves
- What can you take off your pastor's plate?
- How can you help him be more strategic and productive?
- What can you say or do to make your pastor feel like more of a success?
- How can you actively and personally appreciate your pastor today?

Elders, you don't need to possess Solomonic wisdom to make a difference in the life of your senior leader. You have legs, teeth, and hands enough to get started.

So, get started. I think you'll find that even little attempts can have a big impact.

Appendix 2

Your Wife Is Not Your Plurality
How Much Should a Pastor Tell His Wife?

EVERY CHURCH LEADER has been there.[1] You arrive home after an excruciating meeting with someone whose life, due to sin or suffering, has become suddenly and painfully complex. Your wife is no dummy. A routine scan of your face and posture tell her you bear an invisible burden. Once the kids are down, she waits for the right moment to ask, "Okay, what's going on?"

The question demonstrates her love for you, but it also betrays an important reality. Once your wife has perceived your burden, she picks up your burden. The trouble is, she's uninformed, and that can add pounds of anxiety to the load she bears.

As an elder or church leader, how should you understand your wife's "security clearance level"? Is there a baseline curiosity about confidential information that mercy should satisfy? Does

1   This appendix appeared previously as Dave Harvey, "How Much Should a Pastor Tell His Wife?," The Gospel Coalition (website), November 29, 2017, https://www.the gospelcoalition.org/article/much-pastor-tell-wife-2/. Reprinted with permission of the Gospel Coalition.

the one-flesh status of marriage grant full access to counseling details? Partial access? Or should there be an impenetrable firewall between your work at church and your wife at home?

Six Ground Rules

What ground rules matter most in knowing what to share? Here are six I've identified through a few decades of trial and (mostly) error.

Roles Matter

When a church hires a pastor or chooses elders, the church pretty much gets a twofer, the leader and the unpaid consultant to whom he is married. The question is not whether they will talk; the question is whether their talk will be governed by wisdom, discretion, and appropriate confidentiality.

Early in ministry, Kimm and I talked. Oh boy, did we talk! Church problems were an entrée we shared at breakfast, lunch, and dinner. Other pastors on our team had the same practice, so we began discussing some questions. What is our understanding of the role of a pastor's wife in our church? Is she a full-access partner in ministry or a wife who flourishes better with less information? What passages speak specifically to what we might say to our spouses about people's struggles? Have we established a ground rule, and has it been adequately conveyed to the church? These deliberations cut a clearer path for a couple to walk when discussing delicate church matters. Kimm and I realized that she was capable of bearing many burdens with appropriate discretion and without being crushed by the emotional load.

My Heart Matters

The way we talk about our pressures reveals our hearts. For some leaders, their marriage is a venting chamber where every fear, offense, and trouble echoes back to their spouse. Recently, a pastor told me, "During my first few years of ministry, oversharing was my only mode of communication." When I asked why, he said, "Problems exposed the junk in my own heart, and I felt like I needed to unload elsewhere." But something bad happened. He noticed his wife's taste for ministry was growing sour. When he sought counsel and prayed, the pastor recognized that he was actually poisoning his wife. By his venting unbelief and craving her sympathy, his wife became a casualty, not a counselor.

Few things say more about the health of our hearts than how we report things when we're frustrated. Can we convey the necessary information without sprinkling our own cynical commentary? Do we protect the motives of those involved when we report on them? Are we seeking help to examine our own hearts? As my pastor-friend discovered, when it comes to discerning what to share with your wife, the heart matters.

The Law Matters

Did you know that the civil law makes a claim on how we handle the information we hear as leaders? A few necessary questions may help clarify our data handling: Did I come by the information that I could share with my wife indirectly or in my role as a counselor? If the latter, is the information protected by penitent privilege? Do I have an obligation to keep matters private in a way that she does not? Are there any mandatory reporting requirements that already determine the path for my reporting?

No pastor wants to complicate his marriage by naively loading legal burdens on it. Leaders need to know what their state laws say about clergy-penitent privilege and mandatory reporting, and they need to ensure that these laws are not unintentionally violated by communication with spouses. If you want to know where the law limits your communication, talk to older pastors and church law experts. Then remember Proverbs 21:23:

> Whoever keeps his mouth and his tongue
>   keeps himself out of trouble.

Church Policy Matters

Wise elder bodies consider the complexity and liabilities of confidentiality and seek to arm their leaders with rules for engaging others. Laws are a help, but pastors can rarely find their notes from that one church-law class in seminary. And if you're as far removed from your seminary experience as I am, you know the laws have probably changed anyway. Once again, questions are the first step: What is the general policy for the elders on confidentiality? How does the confidentiality policy apply to elders' wives? What would be acceptable information to share, and what would be considered off-limits—and how is that determination made? Can elders gain permission for their wives to be included on details from counseling cases or elders' meetings?

Discretion is a beautiful word, but what it means to "be discreet" is pretty subjective. Moving general encouragements toward specific policies and converting cultural assumptions into written guidelines will help you define how discretion is particularized in each local church.

Maturity Matters

Leaders need to gauge and discern whether or not their spouses have the personal maturity and spiritual health to manage when the curtains are pulled back on the church's brokenness. A mature wife can bear the weight of confidentiality without indiscrete leaks or evenings lost in a forest of anxiety. A spouse who is growing in spiritual health will not be easily unsettled or quickly affronted when she discovers that sin stinks like day-old fish. Love your wife by knowing her and what she's wired to handle. If you want to calculate her maturity level, simply test what happens when her character meets the demands of confidentiality. That's a critical dial on the dashboard of discretion.

Temptation Matters

Distinct from maturity is temptation. What are the vulnerable points of my wife's soul? Does she compartmentalize well, or is she susceptible to fear? Is she prone to instinctive and vocal self-righteousness when struggles and sin surface? Is my wife tempted toward gossip or repeating matters (Prov. 17:9)?

Temptations can be reduced by wise words. Zack Eswine recommends the practice of "general venting."[2] It starts with a leader telling his wife there's something on his mind: "If I seem stressed, it's not you!" Then, offer a general category for the situation: "I have a critic on my mind, and it hurts," or "There's a couple who's struggling, and I'm concerned." Finally, give an invitation

2   Zack Eswine, "What Should Ministry Leaders Share with Their Spouses? Guidelines for Venting," The Pastor's Abbey (blog), May 8, 2017, https://zackeswine.com/what-should-pastors-share-with-their-spouses-guidelines-for-venting/.

to intimacy: "The details won't be helpful, but would you mind if we prayed together?" This approach allows confidentiality to be upheld without the wife feeling excluded.

No Easy Matter

As you can tell, finding the intersection where healthy burden bearing meets prudent discretion is no easy journey. Ground rules help, but for couples trying to find their path, nothing replaces wisdom. So let's end by remembering this potent promise: "If any of you lacks wisdom, let him ask God, who gives generously to all without reproach, and it will be given him" (James 1:5).

Appendix 3

What's the Best Way for a Pastor to Negotiate His Salary?

IT CAN BE AWKWARD for a pastor to talk about his salary. Annual incomes are, after all, the things of earth—unspiritual and unbecoming—far from the meditations of the heavenly minded minister. Or so it seems. Why not just parade the pastor's sex life before the elders too!

In the world of wages, pastors inhabit some pretty conflicted space. On the one hand, a pastor must "manage his own household well" (1 Tim. 3:4). This certainly includes managing his family finances in such a way that bills are paid and the kids are clothed, fed, and able to travel in a dependable car that was made in the twenty-first century. On the other hand, a pastor must not be "a lover of money" (1 Tim. 3:3). We can expect enough (1 Cor. 9:8–11), yet we can't be "greedy for gain" (Titus 1:7). The church should desire an unmuzzled pastor (1 Tim. 5:18), but can the pastor determine what "muzzled" means? Those distinctions are far easier to espouse than to discern.

It's the *salary strain*, an occupational hazard that seems to come with ministry. If navigated unwisely, it can introduce suspicion and stall the church's momentum toward the future. So what's the best way for a pastor to negotiate his salary?

Six Thoughts

Here are six thoughts I hope will be helpful for you. Salary negotiations move toward wisdom when the pastor knows the following:

1. When he knows that money talk always involves heart issues (Matt. 6:21). One's salary is not a unique, amoral, heart-free zone where our desires or fears become suddenly irrelevant. The pastor should speak to God first and often when negotiating his salary. This will help him approach the process as a disciple desiring to receive God's provision and not as a professional seeking to grab what he can.

2. When the pastor knows the church is neither suffering nor being excessively frugal in the offer extended to him. As shepherds in God's church, we are never ambivalent over how the church's spending affects the church's stability. Yet we also don't want to feel like the church is saving money at a cost to our families. If your salary triggers concern on either side of this tension, consider it an invitation from the Holy Spirit for further discussion. In some cases, it may even be a reason to decline a role.

Also, don't become unnecessarily distracted by the salary figure; remember to look at the whole package. Certain benefits such as health/dental/vision insurance, life and disability insurance, retirement, and book and/or cell phone allowances can represent up to another 35–45 percent of the offer. That's real money and represents a loud statement to anyone with ears to hear.

One caveat for the guy preparing to accept his first ministry role. Don't get your hopes too high over what you just read about benefits. God rarely invites men into ministry roles where some kind of financial faith is not required.

3. When the pastor knows how churches assign value *to ministry roles.* From a church standpoint, the factors most often influencing salary offers include

- the size of the church and its budget;
- the church's geographic location—there are significant salary-range differences between US regions;
- the experience of the pastor in relation to the roles and responsibilities of the position;
- comparability to the salaries of other pastors in similar roles;
- equity and fairness of the overall compensation structure of the church staff; and
- the skill sets the pastor brings to the role.

A quick thought on the last one: A pastor being considered may be a remarkably gifted teacher but lack organizational, administrative, and/or strategic-thinking skills. This means the church may need to allocate other staff to cover these weaknesses or underdeveloped skills, thereby altering the value of the role.

4. When the pastor knows his income may grow if the church grows and may shrink if the church experiences hard times. These realities are neither carnal nor unfair but are simply a slice of real life in the local church. In my thirty-five years of ministry, I've been in times of both growth and decline. I've taken salary raises; I've declined raises; I've endured deductions; and I've disputed benefits. Through all these seasons I've discovered that the local church is a dynamic, resilient, vulnerable, organized organism.

Salary offers should be accompanied by seatbelts. By accepting the role, you agree to buckle up and adapt to the unpredictable adventures ahead.

Also, if you're moving from the private sector to a church-staff role, there's a high probability you have a substantial salary reduction coming your way—possibly 40–60 percent. Consider yourself forewarned, but know that it's not personal. It's just one of the many differences between for-profit and nonprofit organizations. And it's one of the sacrifices God invites us to make to serve his people.

5. *When the pastor knows the offer accompanies the faith and enthusiasm of those extending it.* This is just obvious street smarts. If the church's leadership team or search committee is not excited about you in the role, or your arrival is going to divide the church, perhaps it's wiser to keep looking. Yes, God may call some men to churches where their doctrine or vision may polarize the people. But you'd better be certain there is a committed core of gospel-loving, doctrinally driven, courageous folk who are going to support you through the coming storm. Absent that, you're merely postponing your job search for another twelve to eighteen months and eliminating a solid reference from your last place of employment.

6. *When the pastor knows he should communicate gratitude for the offer, even if he is unable to accept it.* More than one person, perhaps many, undoubtedly spent time collaborating to pull together this offer. A wise candidate will appreciate the effort even if he cannot accept the position or salary.

A Brief Word for Elders

Most of you who are elders have an unenviable job. You wish your board role were situated in a well-financed, for-profit company so that salaries did not have the constraints of a church. But in the church, providence, wisdom, reliable comparisons, and tight budgets determine the borders of your generosity. Here are a few things to keep in mind:

- Be honest and transparent about the process for setting, raising, or reducing your pastor's salary or benefits.
- Use the salary-setting discussion to communicate not only your expectations but also your commitment to your pastor's success (see 5 above).
- Discuss the whole package so your pastor understands the value and significance of each benefit.
- Don't allow the instincts of thrifty elders to determine the culture of salary setting or salary reviews. When conducting salary reviews, be as generous as performance and wisdom allow.
- Lavish your pastor with encouragement throughout the year so that your statement of support is not reduced to what happens with his salary.
- Appoint an elder to take point in caring for your pastor, including an annual inquiry about the financial health of his family. If he is struggling, arrange for financial consultation.
- Pray that God blesses your pastor spiritually and financially in unexpected ways. It means a great deal to pastors when they know their elders pray for their needs.

Back to Pastors: Payday and the Last Day

As you seek to navigate these tensions, do so remembering this remarkable reality: The final reward for your role is not delivered in your monthly paycheck. Ultimately, you serve the church with another day in view. "And when the chief Shepherd appears, you will receive the unfading crown of glory" (1 Pet. 5:4).

Pastor or pastoral candidate, as you negotiate your salary, remember the unfading crown of glory. Let it inspire your humility and restrain your entitlement. Let it fill every salary discussion (or dispute!) with the knowledge that there is no sacrifice for God made in the present that will not be richly compensated by God in the future.

Appendix 4

Term Limits for Elders?

Jeff Robinson

SHOULD ELDERS IN THE LOCAL CHURCH be subject to term limits, or is election to the board by the body, or by the elders (depending upon one's polity), more like joining the US Supreme Court, a lifetime appointment? For the church I serve the answer is yes and no.

Scripture is silent on this issue, so it's important to say there's no "biblical view" of term limits for elders. Local church leaders have freedom to answer this question, and the answers are surely debatable. Godly wisdom and biblical principles should be our guide.

I answer "yes and no" not to be coy or provocative but because I believe term limits should apply to lay elders and not to staff elders. Lay elders are elected church leaders who are not paid by the church. Their service is rendered strictly on a volunteer basis, while staff elders are typically vocational ministers who earn at least part of their living through pay from the church.

I do think it's wise for lay elders to serve limited terms. This is the practice at my church and many others led by a plurality of elders. In our church—and this seems to be fairly standard—lay elders may serve consecutive three-year terms (thus six years) before they must rotate off the board for at least one year. After the first three years, they must be reaffirmed by the church by a congregational vote, and our lay elders are given the opportunity to step away from the board for a year in between the three-year terms, if they deem it necessary, and return for a second three-year term thereafter. After two consecutive three-year terms, a lay elder will automatically rotate off for at least one year.

Why do our elders think term limits are wise? Mainly for these practical/pragmatic reasons:

1. Scripture doesn't teach "once an elder always an elder." I've heard the argument (and sympathize with it on a level) that a God-called man never ceases to be called. But churches are dynamic organisms where change happens to the congregation and in the lives of the elders who serve there. We feel it's wise, therefore, to have ways for men to step away without confusing people over whether they are abandoning their life appointment.

2. Limits prevent burnout. As a vocational pastor, I know all too well the rigors of ministry. It can be awfully tough to lead a congregation and can leave a leader spiritually, mentally, and physically drained. In the same way running a car's engine without oil can burn it up, running an elder year after year without adequate time off can lead to a breakdown. Time away from serving allows for healing and rest.

3. Limits for some elders, but not all, help protect the institutional history and continuity through the elders that remain.

4. Limits can help keep high an elder board's effectiveness. As Jonathan Leeman at 9Marks puts it, term limits "allow the older gentleman whose work, let's just say, is not what it used to be" to roll off the board.

What about vocational elders? Don't they need a break, too? Most definitely. Elders who are on the church's payroll, particularly the lead pastor, need to be given regular sabbaticals so they don't flame out over the long haul. As one of my friends puts it, he must "come away so he doesn't come apart."

There are disadvantages to term limits as well. A man can be in the midst of a good work when the time arrives for him to rotate off. This is why churches have the freedom to answer this question for themselves according to what works best in their circumstances, and I have known of churches that don't have term limits and have functioned that way with significant effectiveness and unity.

General Index

Scripture Index

THE GOSPEL **COALITION**

The Gospel Coalition is a fellowship of evangelical churches deeply committed to renewing our faith in the gospel of Christ and to reforming our ministry practices to conform fully to the Scriptures. We have committed ourselves to invigorating churches with new hope and compelling joy based on the promises received by grace alone through faith alone in Christ alone.

We desire to champion the gospel with clarity, compassion, courage, and joy—gladly linking hearts with fellow believers across denominational, ethnic, and class lines. We yearn to work with all who, in addition to embracing our confession and theological vision for ministry, seek the lordship of Christ over the whole of life with unabashed hope in the power of the Holy Spirit to transform individuals, communities, and cultures.

Through its pastoral resources, The Gospel Coalition aims to encourage and equip current and prospective pastors for faithful endurance over a lifetime of ministry in the church. By learning from experienced ministers of different ages, races, and nationalities, we hope to grow together in godly maturity as the Spirit leads us in the way of Jesus Christ.

Join the cause and visit TGC.org for fresh resources that will equip you to love God with all your heart, soul, mind, and strength, and to love your neighbor as yourself.

TGC.org

Also Available from the Gospel Coalition

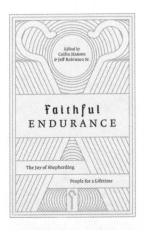

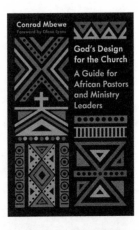

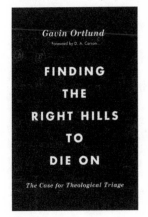

For more information, visit **crossway.org**.